CK Ford Media Pre

MW01027801

"MIRACLE ZONES"

Book 2 of *The Waters of Life Chronicles*

By: C.K. FORD

Author, Speaker, Inspirational Teacher, Mentor, &
Intuitive Counselor

CK Ford Media

www.CKFord.Online

"Miracle Zones": Book 2 of The Waters of Life Chronicles"

Published by: **C.K.Ford Media:**

Address: P.O. Box 44, Clarkston, GA 30021

Publication Imprint: CK\Ford#Media,
United States

Website: www.CKFord.Online

Copyright © 2021 -- C.K. FORD Media

Email: cfordinspires@gmail.com

Address: CK Ford Media,

P.O. Box 44, Clarkston, GA 30021

ISBN: 978-1-7361842-3-3 (Print / Paperback)

ISBN: 978-1-7361842-4-0 (E-Book / Digital)

Printed and Manufactured in the United States of America

*** Cover Art Graphics Designer: Mr. James F. DiLuzio**

Acknowledgements:

First and foremost—I give thanks, honor, and gratitude unto the Almighty Divine (the Lord of Creation), as the works of my hands and labors of Spirit are made possible. I am thankful for life, liberty, and the Hope of My Calling.

To my remarkable daughters **A.J. and A.M.** (the magnificent A- Team) for their unfailing love. You both are a true inspiration, shining brightly and excelling in everything that you set your minds and hearts to do; it is such an honor to be your mother. Thanks for striving to be the absolute best of who you were to created to be, forging your own paths, thus making an indelible mark upon the world. I am a better person because of you!

To my amazing Father, _Mr. J.E. Ford_-- who set the bar high by overcoming and mastering every challenge head on, without ever missing a beat; always leading by example in ethics, character, integrity, and steadfast commitment of being true to who he is-- no more, no less. Thank you for being the Greatest of All Times, the stuff that legends are made of!!

Special Thanks to all the extraordinary women who blazed the trails before me—fearless, daring, and tenacious, never allowing the obstacles to sideline you. Also, to all those that are to come along after me—do not be afraid to dream and follow your passion, because your voice matters!

A note of gratitude and thanksgiving to the Universe for all the marvelous opportunities that are to come; also, to my ancestors for paving the way that I may come forth for such a time as this. It is their shoulders that I now stand upon. As my journey continues, I carry the torch to light and the way, helping lead others out of the darkness and despair, in the personal quest of self-discovery, ushering them into the hope of their calling.

Namaste '

* Thanks to Mr. JF Diluzio, for creating such a breathtaking book cover! Your work speaks for itself...

PREFACE

Regardless of where you find yourself, allow this book to lead you into your NOW MOMENT of Truth. **"Miracle Zones"** is a journey with Spirit into my private and very personal moments of truth, line upon line, page upon page. Through my personal encounters with Spirit / God / Universe, one day at a time, the hope, truth, and commitment of my calling emerges.

"Miracle Zones" is the second book of **The Waters of Life Chronicles Series—** a collection of journals and entries depicting / highlighting my times of faith, fellowship, Devotion, and deep conversations with God. At the time, of these writings and journal entries, I had no plans of making my private writings public, considering that these were "transcriptions" received by way of prayer and meditation. Yet, as we go about diligently doing the things that are so much a part of who we are in faith, the Faithfulness of Our Creator has plans far greater than we are able to conceive or Imagine. It is my hope that this book serves as inspiration to all who partake of it, that you may come to a space of Deep Intimacy with Spirit—gaining clearer insight, wisdom, and understanding of YOUR PURPOSE. Allow yourself to experience the beauty and splendor of Spirit, speaking to your heart and Soul, the core of your Existence through the pages of this book.

Dare to embark upon your personal quest and discovery of all that you are, have been, and will be throughout your life, as Spirit invites you to enter in and embrace the God / Goddess that you have always been from the beginning of Creation. This Personalized Invitation is ALL- INCLUSIVE without expiration date.

So, WELCOME HOME, as you are greeted by the angels and The God of The Universe who has been anticipating your Grand Arrival!! Step in and partake of your "**Miracle Zones**" Adventure... Allow "The Waters of Life" to quench your dehydrated Soul...

INTRODUCTION

Greetings! So glad that you stopped what you were doing to take a few moments just to BREATHE and commune with the Universe, giving Thanks and Gratitude for where you are right now. (Imagine if this were God / Spirit speaking to you)

Welcome to my world, as I introduce you to not only my works, but a bird's eye view and glimpses into my conversations with God / Spirit. Each day, in my fellowship, meditation, devotion, and prayer time, I breathed deeply and released whatever came from my heart and soul... albeit in times of distress, frustration, and a myriad of dilemmas in life. I would sit in places of quiet or would find the space of inner solitude to silence all of the chatter and distractions, problems, and busyness of life just to navigate and process everything that was going on in my world. After having said and released all of the internal heaviness until there were no more words left to say, then I pressed in deeper to just LISTEN.

Through purposeful LISTENING and purposeful resolve, I would begin to HEAR the Spirit of God speak from within. It's one thing to LISTEN, yet something much greater transpires as I was compelled to WRITE and take note of everything that was being spoken as I was hearing it from the Realms of Spirit. There was no time to process or second guess, I was required to listen as the words came and write as fast and furiously as was being spoken to me from an energetic realm that was far BEYOND ME. The time to read what had been poured into / through me from Spirit would not come about until afterwards, sometimes hours afterwards or at time the next day. Though labor intensive, at the time, it never occurred to me that what I deemed to be mere journals, are now the manifested creations of Spirit--

destined to be released years later as a series: "The Waters of Life Chronicles"—"*Miracle Zones*" becoming Book 2 of this series.

Great Thanks to you-- for the time that is being set aside to sit in your own quiet space with Spirit, to both discover and uncover those hidden places from within your soul, that you may give voice and recognition to the Greatness that is resident at your core of existence—Wisdom and Truth Embodiment of The God of Grace Eternal; your Peace, Hope, Protection, and Provision of Ages...

"Partitioned Arrivals"

Chipping away at those unsealed cracks,
That were supposed to be masked over---
Unreachable and untouchable, yet pushed back…

Denied and hidden unto this new season emerged,
Changes or continuity? Perhaps on the verge of,
Something that was missed,
While spiraling beyond the abyss,
Deep inside the silence of things profound,
Sanctity of Solitude resounding,
Amidst the Thunder and Stars.

Though time did not halt,
The dams that were built to protect from the floods,
Somehow in the distances hearing *Teardrops of BLOOD,*
Broke all barriers and transcended the Impossible,
Then the odds not only turned favorable,
But tangible beyond Recognition!

Excavation of Sacred land,
Yields treasures unknown, while before long,
The beauty is unmasked, glowing with brilliance,
Far too prevalent for those naked eyes and forlorn hearts,
To not forever be awakened, enamored, softened,
Enlightened-
In heightened expectancy of the delightfully strange,
Beyond comparison of the stable or deranged…
Carefully examined through cautious eyes,
What was once deemed as foolish notions,
Are now confounding those worldly wise!

After the rise and fall of the tides,
Peace creeps in just to vacation for a while,
Then clarity seeks Companions and Friends,

Those once insidious Visions that birth…
The manifestations of Glory, Splendor, and
TOTAL SURRENDER,
While beckoning the Lost unto the light of,
That Welcoming Newfound Home!

Written: Monday, 05 July 2004 @ 0245 Hours

Monday Morning
22 September 2003 @ 0905 Hours

Hallelujah! Many are the afflictions of the righteous, but the Lord Almighty delivers us from them all. This is a day of Divine Interventions and Miraculous Setups, as Our Forever Faithful God shows up, with the company of angels, and has so freely given us the Spirit of Wisdom and Peace WITHIN to set the records straight- righting all wrongs that have been done unto those who worship God Almighty in Spirit and Truth! There is healing, deliverance, restoration, and breakthroughs in the land. I- Almighty Divine am not concerned about mine peoples' comforts but focus on the condition of their hearts and spirits. When the hearts, spirits, minds, and mouths are operating outside of Divine Alignment, then there shall be no comforts to indulge in, declares the Lord of Hosts.

Truly, I say unto all who have an ear to hear, that whosoever will, let them come into their Most Holy Place with all that they are, withholding nothing. All who are hard-pressed, heavy laden, burdened, anxious, stressed, depressed, oppressed, sick in the mind or body, financially distressed, and even the lonely, let them come, declares the Lord God Almighty. Whenever they come, I will have them to drink from the fountains of Living Water that they may never thirst or hunger again. They who seek first the Wisdom of the Kingdom of God and all righteousness, (*being in right standing within themselves, abiding in peace and wholeness*), then surely everything that is needed shall be provided for without fail.

In all of thy getting, seek to gain understanding. They who receive the Words of Truth with no revelation knowledge are unable to advance, or to come out of pits of entrapment. No stone is left unturned, and all that has been done out of spite will be made null and void. The vessels that I – God

Almighty have created in masculine form, possess physical strength, yet many times may fall prey to mental torment and disillusionment and causing them to become spiritually weak from the battles of the mind, for they are unaware and not fully awake. Oftentimes, they are too easily distracted, persuaded, and enticed by the woes of the flesh.

Let every man who desires marriage, and seeks to find himself a good partner, seek not of the desires of the flesh, but that which is Spirit and Truth. Therefore, and when he finds a godly counterpart of virtue, courage, faith, and noble character, he has found himself a good thing and receives great favor in the eyes of the Lord. However, before seeking out a mate, each person to strive to be of impeccable character, that they may recognize and accept the blessing when it is presented to them. Wherefore, it is wise to do the necessary work on oneself, thus becoming the best person and partner to a counterpart at the proper time, rather than to create chaos, havoc, and upheaval in the lives of others. Strive to become the person who is peaceable in spirit and a blessing to dwell with, rather than making stringent demands of others that you would not be able uphold if under the same pressures.

Above all things, allow your no to be no and your yes to be yes, for a double-minded person is unstable in all of his / her ways. Go about thy livelihood in a manner that promotes peace, kindness, generosity, while abiding in Truth and Love. When seeds of discord are sown into the lives of others, there shall be no rest for the weary. A house divided always crumbles, while a person divided in heart and intentions bring torment upon themselves. However, the season is swiftly approaching where they shall undergo in-depth training and vigorous discipleship to learn the language and precepts of covenant loyalty, faithfulness, and how misuse and improper distribution of confidential information can lead to self-destruction. It is time for the Sons and Daughters of God to rise up out of their squalor, taking their rightful place, space, and positions of Kingdom Authority and recognize that I am God Almighty who abides within the depths of their existence. For Gods and Goddesses of The Creator who abide in the shadows of the Almighty is your Hope of Glory and shall not feast on the bread of shame.

The days of Miraculous Interventions have arrived. For those who have been praying against the chosen, appointed servants of Almighty Divine, while throwing rocks and hiding their hands shall reap what they have sown. They will be made to learn valuable lessons that they could not grasp any other way, unless they had made both a mockery and ridicule of mine precious, mature Sons and Daughters. Those who have been found guilty in the spilling their fellow sisters and brothers' blood, they bring about torment upon themselves. Repentance of such misdeeds is prerequisite! Yet, vengeance is mine, says the Lord. Mine precious people are to take heart, lift up their heads, and send up praises unto me, the Lord of Hosts, while looking neither to the left or the right. They are to look only unto me, the Lord of Hosts, for I am brighter than the North Star. For I am Jehovah Jireh: Almighty Provider. I am Divine Health, Healing, Deliverance, Hope, Strength, Help, and Wisdom. I am also the Kinsman Redeemer throughout humanity. *(Moment of Meditation)* …

My precious people have embarked upon the **Miracle Zones** for their lives. I am Jehovah God- Thy Strong Tower and Fortress indeed. I have come to reveal new things that supersede previous visions and limitations. Take off all limits, and I shall grant and impart unto my people the power to create and receive wealth untold through **Wisdom Principles** from the Spirit Realms and obtain trifold, multi-dimensional harvests. *Write the visions and make them plain on tablets, for the visions are yet for an appointed time and that appointed time is NOW, exclaims the Lord of Hosts!*

Keep careful watch and ears to the Spirit of God, as revelations come forth. Those that have been haughty, condescending, and have attempted to make a mockery of my people in their present situations, surely their words shall revisit them right where they live. The haughty shall be leveled and brought down in humility. Even though I brought them up out of pits, declares God, and given them avenues of income, they have now forgotten where they came from while continuing to bite of the hands of those that have fed them, and kicking their kindred ones while they are down. They suffer because of the works of their own hands and misdeeds they have done unto others. Their utter undoing shall come through the making of their own hands. They will go through the fire and storms that they may be purified from the inside out as they repent. As they are then purged through the process, being consecrated, and purified by the trials of life, there shall be nothing left except that which is true, authentic, pure, and genuine. As they stand face to face with the Spirit of Truth that is to be revealed from within, having a heart of true of repentance, the Spirit of Restoration shall come forth to rebuild them with care and diligence, they shall become committed and steadfast to the Lord of Hosts for longevity of days.

Hallelujah Anyhow! The Spirit of the Lord has come to set the captives free. They that have a mind of God and Holy Spirit Fortitude are to uplift those who are weaker, to bring about empowerment- that they may receive and abide in Revelation Knowledge, for the equipping of understanding in the growth process of Divinity's plans, purposes, and precepts. Let the Spirit of the Lord arise within the hearts of the people of God, in bringing about order and supernatural restoration again to those who shall flourish in their houses, families, and livelihoods. No more going astray, for the death of old things shall swiftly come, while the dead shall be left to bury its own. (*Moment of Meditation*) ...

Praise the Lord of Hosts for the scattering of the enemies, wreckage of unclean territories, and the cleansing of all that is impure and unjust. I am the Lord God Almighty and the where the Spirit of the Lord is, there is Truth, Liberty and Justice that the people may abide in Peace and Wholeness. The death of the old things shall catapult new life and restoration. Mourn not! Celebrate the victorious arrivals, for I AM Jehovah God Divine, who has made ultimate proclamations from beginning to end! *Amen*

Tuesday Morning
23 September 2003 @ 0630 Hours

Hallelujah Anyhow! Today, declares the Lord of Hosts, is a day for recompense to come forth and amends to be made for all wrong doings. Let all of those who profess to have a relationship with God, lift up his hands in examination for blood. *(Moment of Meditation)* ...

I am God and by the Renewing of the Minds through the Holy Spirit, the captives are set free. Therefore, there will be no excuses made for lapses in judgment, for when people have been provided with wise counsel they may not wander aimlessly, wallowing in foolishness, or taking stabs in the dark, only to come out with blood on their hands. Therefore, with increased knowledge comes greater responsibility!

Why must they mindlessly rebuke all Divine Instruction? Perhaps, they choose death over life because they feel unworthy of Greater Purpose for their lives. It is uncanny, declares the Lord of Hosts, why they choose to wallow in rebellion and dwell in debauchery as thieves, idolaters, perverse, and pious, when they have been hand selected to have Dominion and Authority in The Kingdom of God. However, dearly beloved ones, the battles do not belong to my Mature Sons and Daughters; they are to trust and believe that I- the Lord God Almighty have equipped them with everything necessary to stand in the face of adversity, and they shall be victorious as the Word of the Lord is sent out ahead of them causing every obstacle to be demolished! Wherefore, my precious Sons and Daughters are Gods and Goddesses within the Earth Realm to operate with impact and influence within their livelihoods.

Unto mine precious hand-select, whom I have set apart for Profound Purpose, seemingly in lonely places so that I may prepare them for greatness and glory, ARISE! For those who have been given much, greater degrees of responsibility is also required of them in return. Although they are mocked, ridiculed, minimized, and demeaned- I have created these prized vessels as peculiar people. Let not the words from the mouths of evildoers nor the blows from their hands throw my people off course. Wherefore, distractions may lead to destruction!! *(Moment of Meditation)* ...

Despair not, declares the Lord of Hosts, for almost suddenly, my people shall look for the enemy and the enemy shall not be found. The enemies of your souls tend to do themselves in, when my people operate within the Divine Purposes, doing what is right and just to the best of their abilities. Through these processes, my people are avenged on every side. However, my people are not to gloat over the tragedies and downfalls of others yet remain steadfast in prayer and supplication for the families of those who have come to destruction. Whatever has been done to the least of my chosen children has also been done unto me. No stone shall be left unturned because the Spirit of the Lord God Almighty has come to set the records straight and establish Divine Order in the land.

I am the Lord of Hosts and I neither sleep nor slumber. All power, grace, and authority to heal My People everywhere they are hurting has been poured out in droves. Yet, those who have dealt harshly with fellow humanity and have assaulted my children in the spirit, body, and mind shall surely reap as they have sown. Although many have wallowed in haughtiness and remain deceived in thinking they are justified in what they have done. No matter what the circumstance and situations dictate, I- the Lord God Almighty have sent forth bands of angels to take up the plights of my Sons and Daughters whom worship me in spirit and in truth.

Rejoice, dear people of God Most High, for your miracle seasons have arrived. Although you have been battered and broken in spirit, I am your Creator and you shall not do without any good thing. ***On this day, be still and know that I am God! I AM bringing you out of the shadows, into the spotlight and use you mightily to confound the wise and cocky.*** Hold on- for the change is about to arrive and the breakthrough is at your door. Behold, proclaims Lord of Hosts- grace and wealth abounding are seeking you out and everything that was previously delayed and denied will be turned around in your favor. The Wisdom of God produces the FAVOR of God! *(Moment of Meditation) ...*

In all things, allow your no to be no and your yes to be yes! Truly, a double-minded person is unstable in all of his / her ways. As my precious people continue on the path of righteousness, working out their own salvation with reverence and understanding, Wisdom, Truth, and Peace. I am God and I have not brought my people thus far to leave them. Therefore, believe me at my word, for my promises are yes and amen to they who abide in the Spirit of Truth and Peace. I am the Lord thy God and I have never seen the righteous forsaken or my children out begging for bread.

Shackles will fall off, eyes will be opened, and miracles will pour forth. The fruits of the land are overflowing and the harvests of those that have fasted and prayed in purity of heart shall abound. Standfast and see the salvation and wonders of Almighty God. This is miracle day and recompense hour, so be not hard-hearted and forgive others as I have forgiven you. Yet, my people are not required to be foolish in reconnecting with those who seek to do them harm nor abide in toxicity, which is putrid to the soul.

Amen.

Wednesday Morning
24 September 2003 @ 0635 Hours

Glory unto the Lord God on High, for awesome and marvelous are the amazing works indeed. Praise be unto Almighty God, all people who are troubled, burdened, perplexed, heavy laden, and bound. God Almighty, being the Creator and sustainer of all life form shall lift you up from the trenches and ditches, placing your feet on a rock that shall not crumble. For truly, **Yeshua** is the rock in a weary land, shelter in the times of storm. Magnify and glorify the Spirit of Christ Consciousness, for the ways out of seemingly impossible situations have been made!

Rejoice, declares the Lord of Hosts. For I have declared the end from the beginning and the beginning from the end. So, let not my people be anxious for anything or stress over how the miracles shall come about. Be still and know that I AM God, and I shall do exceeding, abundantly, beyond all that my people could ever ask or think according to the Holy Spirit Power that abides within you. Truly, I say unto my most precious people of The True Living God, you were not brought to this dark place to be abandoned in the miry pits, but I have brought you to this point so that you may see my miracles manifested like fire and water. Judge ye' not, lest ye be judged. And without faith, it is impossible to please me, declares God Almighty. Let this wilderness experience serve as a test of your faith that shall produce the mightiest of testimonies. Let all they that are for my purposes and precepts, not only stand up and say so, yet also execute the instructions and directions that I have provided. For at this very hour, I, Jehovah God Almighty am deeply grieved and disturbed by the pains that have been inflicted upon my people.
(Moment of Meditation)

In all things, declares the Lord of Hosts, my people are to allow their yes to stand always as a firm yes, and their no's to suffice as a steadfast no. There is no tolerance for wavering in commitments. All things are to be done decently and in Divine Order. Right now, more is out of order than is in order. Therefore, watch carefully as I move so swiftly that it will turn trees upside down, wreck buildings into piles of rubble, and render every assignment of darkness null and void!! Truly, I say unto thee, dearly beloved children, despair not, for I have already lain to ruin the foundations of misdeeds and evils that have been done unto the least of my people. Continue to walk the high road and look neither to the left or right because distractions lead to destruction. Keep your eyes on me, as your ways shall become plain and clear step by step. They that have set out to shame, humiliate, make a mockery of, defile, dishonor, and disrespect you, shall be swallowed up by waves of the their own misdeeds reverberating, that shall revisit havoc and wrath upon the pious and haughty where they have attempted to bury others alive. Their foundations and households shall be laid to ruin, for whatsoever has been sown, shall also be reaped. And that which has been done to the least of them, has also been done unto Jehovah Almighty.

My love and goodness endure forever. I am dismayed, declare the Lord of Hosts. For they know what is right and just yet refusing to abide in Truth and Mercy. They are as lamps with no oil on a dark, stormy night. They refuse to prepare for the times of trouble where obedience to my instructions could have diverted them from encountering disasters. A fool in his/ her folly shall surely self-destruct, while self-destruction is far more painful than being destroyed by freak accidents of nature. When an earthquake comes and the ground opens to swallow up buildings and people, then this could not be avoided.

There is no hiding place, and no stones are left unturned. Those who blatantly defile Holy Ground and the appointed of God, their bones shall ache constantly with no medical explanations to be found as cause. Their insides will be turned inside out and no medicine, except true and absolute repentance shall soothe the pains. They will sleep but never rest; they will work but never have enough and shall indulge in fleshly pleasures only to be rendered spiritually and emotionally bankrupt! What then shall my people say to all these things? Because God is for us, who dares to rise up against us and think that they shall be victorious? *(Moment of Meditation) ...*

No holds will be barred, and surely, the salvation of the Lord shall prevail forever. Let not your hearts be troubled by what you have seen and heard, precious children of Divinity. Because I am God, I shall turn these very situations around in your favor and the enemies of your soul will be demolished and buried right where they live. Behold! On this day, my people shall see my hands manifest miracles and wonders. Inhale, then exhale, for the cycles of needless pain and turmoil are broken and rendered void!

Hallelujah! Amen

Thursday Morning
25 September 2003 @ 0630 Hours

Hallelujah! Truly, it is Restoration Time! So, let everything that have breath, praise the Lord! As we shout with voices of triumph and praise, God is causing all things work together for good of those that abide in Love and are called and sent according to the Greater Purpose. Standing on the brink of new horizons in this day, God shall prove Faithful and True forever more. Therefore, I beseech ye' dear brothers and sisters, that in all things, allow your no to stand as a certain no, and your yes to serve as a definite yes. For God sent forth the Holy Spirit to abide in the even those who are uncommitted—that they may repent, have a change of heart and mind, that they may receive grace and favor abounding. The Holy Spirit was sent forth to right all the wrongs inflicted on the precious people of God, while bringing forth conviction, not condemnation. *(Moment of Meditation)* ...

Grace and Favor abounding are rewards given to those who are faithful, declares God. Let not any person boast specifically of themselves or in their works of piety but boast of the Goodness of God as they abide in the land of the Living. For surely, I say unto thee, that everything that is done out of the darkness shall be brought to light. What does darkness and light have in common? Absolutely nothing! When light floods in, the darkness must flee and is washed away completely. My people, who I have called according to my name, must not consort with the foolish and wicked counselors of this world, declares God. The wicked and foolish may overthrow those who are weaker in the mind and spirit, coercing them to abandon the paths of righteousness, so that they will not walk alone in their folly. The enemy of your souls come to deceive, steal, kill, and destroy. Distractions lead to destruction!! Therefore, the people of God are to keep their eyes and hearts fixed on Divine Truth, that they may be led into all Wisdom and

Revelation Knowledge, rightly dividing fact from fiction. The people have always done what they know how to do at the time, but when they learn better, they are required to do better. After continual efforts are put forth to do better, they should have grown and graduated to doing what is right and just all the time, for this is the outline for growth unmatched.

On this day, prepare for Divine Interventions, Supernatural Manifestations, and powerful revelations to come forth. Do not stand dismayed, for I am the Lord of Hosts and I give unto my precious people the Wisdom of Kingdom Principles as their inheritance, wherefore the gates of darkness and foolishness shall not prevail. Keep your eyes fixed on God Almighty, for there are great and mighty works to be performed. At all times, tell the truth, the whole truth, and nothing but the truth. Just as iron sharpens iron, so does one brother / sister sharpen another. Do not be afraid to ask of me, the Lord of Hosts, those difficult questions and seek wisdom that you may feed others in need. Because I AM God-- I neither sleep nor slumber. Whatever has been done to the least of my children has also been done unto me, the Lord of Hosts. I implore my dearly beloved ones to stand fast as olive trees planted by the rippling waters--- not being moved by what they see because everything that is seen is subject to change. As the branches of my people are being pruned and crushed, the sweet fragrance of Spirit, Truth, and Renewal of priceless oils shall pour out of them while permeating every place that the soles of their feet tread. The steps of the pure at heart Sons and Daughters of God are directed by the Lord Almighty.

Behold precious people of God: I implore you to become not ensnared in circumstances and situations; for a circumstance is only a specific circle that you are standing in the middle of for a particular time and season. *(Moment of Meditation)* ... Haste makes waste and a fool in his / her folly shall soon self-destruct.

Those who abide in cycles of mayhem and foolishness, without impunity—they bring forth the revisiting the disaster upon future generations, unless they repent and turn towards Truth, Wisdom, Mercy, Healing, and Compassion! They who have sown seeds of discord, proven ungrateful, disloyal, dishonest, dishonorable, and disrespectful unto the Lord God Almighty their fellow brothers and sisters of humanity, shall be made to reap what they have sown. Now is the time to make better, more informed decisions of Wisdom, walking in the ways of discipline as to not continue those wash, rinse, and repeat cycles of their misdeeds.

Expect the unexplained and unexpected on this day! Anticipate the arrival of long overdue communications. The walls are being broken down and the consciences are being brought into alignment with the Higher Spirit Consciousness. Turn from wrath and diffuse potentially negative situations with soft answers, for people that do not know different ways are confounded by the Wisdom and Love of God through those who abide unto the Higher Calling of The Divine. The LOVE of God covers a multitude of wrongdoings and prevails over all other things. Let everything that was established on the foundations built by Love, flourish, and those now dead bones that were buried while still alive, then suffocated by the woes of darkness--- are called to Arise! Come Forth, be hereby Resurrected, and LIVE AGAIN!!! No stone shall be left unturned as the sun breaks through the darkness of night.

Hallelujah! Amen.

Saturday Morning
27 September 2003 @ 1140 Hours

Hallelujah! Great and mighty are the works of God indeed. We are called to worship the Lord in Spirit and in Truth, wherefore, anything less is purely unacceptable. This is a day of Divine Interventions, Seasons of Breakthrough and Supernatural Change. In this very hour, the thing that is essential for all other changes to take place is the changing of the mindsets. Mediocrity settles for whatever is offered, but greatness spans the miles and runs the course to seek new dimensions, while going past all previous limitations. The thing that determines what one shall have is how far one is willing to go while being stretched and processed for the Glorious Purpose of God in their lives – which is the illuminated path into their *Miracle Zones*!

Behold, shouts the Lord of Hosts! On this day, I will prove unto my people that Love and Truth prevails for those who follow the guidance that I set forth for their lives. All that I have promised shall be transferred into my peoples' hands suddenly. God Almighty- The Great I AM, makes no idle promises. Whatsoever I have decreed, it is already in existence, although may not yet be tangible. Therefore, dare to believe me at my word while abiding in reverence unto Me. Loved ones are being brought out of captivity and restored to their rightful place in who they were created to be! They may have previously been on the run, proclaims God, but there is no hiding place, for I abide within the depths of their being. They shall not escape the power and infinite mercies of the Holy Spirit, the dozens of angels, the calling, appointments, and Divine Purposes of God upon their lives, the power of praying families and covenant partnerships.

I am God, yet I did not connect and join my people in covenant partnerships because the way would be easy. I have

declared that whosoever I have placed my people in covenant with shall stand, stand, and stand some more. For in having done all that one can do, they are to stand on the Word that I -- God Almighty have spoken to and within them. For the effectual, steadfast prayers of the Sons and Daughters of God shall produce abundance of fruit. Covenant partnerships are not based on how one feels, but based on principles, precepts, and decrees of Truth. My promises are not rendered null and void even though the rebellious think that they have the options to change their minds and walking through doors that I have said are to be closed to outsiders.
(Moment of Meditation) ...

I am the Lord of Hosts. I am not a man that I should lie, nor the Son of Man that I should repent. Therefore, shout GRACE, GRACE! into the situations, leave them alone, and watch the works of the Lord God Almighty. The victory and triumph shall be hasty and nearly instantaneous!

Divine Appointments are nearby. Therefore, continue to walk in My Divine Will and purposes that I have established for you, as Divine Connections seek you out. The vision is yet for the appointed time and that appointed time is NOW. Divine Revelation of TRUTH is imparted unto those who diligently seek. I send loved ones from the other side of the world to both facilitate and implement creative abilities, while being partakers of miracles in the lives of my people. Bear not false witness because those who strike pledges in secret against the children of God shall be dealt with in urgency. May the words of my peoples' mouth and meditation of their hearts be pleasing and acceptable at all times, for I am the Lord of Hosts. Each word that is spoken brings something into creation. Therefore, choose to speak wisely as to not become ensnared by the fruits of your lips.

Repair, refurbishing, and restoration come by way of grace unlimited. Lift up your Holy Hands and shout Hallelujah, for

I am God of the wealthy and poor. Standfast! This is a day of miracles and awesome dimensions. Be of peace and good cheer, bearing witness to all that I have performed in the here and now, for I am the Lord Jehovah.

Amen

Sunday Morning
28 September 2003 @ 0840 Hours

All praise and thanksgiving for this day! Hallelujah! God I AM is Forever Faithful, and proven to bestow mercy and grace, while calling life into every dead thing that was once fruitful. The Spirit of God declares:

"On this day, I will pour out my spirit upon all humanity. Because I AM God, I shall gift you the nations as your inheritance. For it is not by might or by power, but by My Spirit, that people who have wronged others shall be called unto total repentance and made to pay restitution to those whom they have spitefully used, misused, and abused. The wages of our warfare are not carnal, but spiritual and mighty in the pulling down of strongholds. On this day, the people whom I call by my name shall see my grace, glory, and goodness abound.

As the righteousness of God is called to worship the Lord, thy God is Spirit and in Truth, the harvest is bountiful, for those have walked in commitment as to the proportion of their faith and measure of their understanding. Half-witted, non-committals, "faking it to fit in" attitudes are completely unacceptable. Therefore, declares God, my people should allow their no to stand as a steadfast no, and their yes to be vehemently yes. Double-mindedness is not of kingdom standards, for a double-minded person is unstable in all of his / her ways. This day marks the day of Divine Shifting, for everything that was out of order shall be swiftly catapulted into alignment by way of Spirit and Truth.

Be prepared, for the things that my people least expect are the very things that will transpire. All will know and understand on this day that all things work together for the good of they that are called, sent, and obedient to the purposes of God for their lives. Grace, Grace, the Amazing Grace of the Lord God Almighty is working out all the kinks to make every crooked place straight. Forgiveness, faithfulness, humility, and submission unto God shall be the sustaining factors that mark the character of the virtuous people of the Most High God. When my people do not waver in their commitments unto me, I- the Lord of Hosts pave the way for all things to be made anew. As surely as grace has brought my people thus far, my grace and mercy are more than sufficient, and shall lead them on even further. Rejoice! I am the Lord Almighty and My Goodness and Favor is poured out upon my people. They reigns of terror are over and hereby burned at the stakes, never to rise out of the ashes again.

My faithful Sons and Daughters are to exercise mercy while walking in Love because I have sanctioned them to walk the higher roads at all times. This factor is utilized to prepare my committed, honorable ones for greatness and favor unprecedented. Careful, forewarns God!! Guard your heart and allow my Spirit Leading and Grace to flow through you like raging rivers, for I am the Lord your God. I have made ways possible when you could not fathom the way based on your understanding. When my people crucify their flesh and silence the inner voice of self-criticism and condemnation, they shall reap the good of the land. No matter what happens, I am still God and far greater than all of your circumstances and situations, leaving no stone unturned.

The **Miracle Zone** is being unraveled. I have pruned and pressed my people so that the oil of the of their very essence shall be purified and pour out like cascading waterfalls. Be still and know that I AM God within the very fiber of your being. Shout Hallelujah! The effectual fervent prayers of those who worship God in Spirit and Truth avail much.

Amen

Monday Morning
29 September 2003 @ 0220 Hours

Glory unto the Lord on High! God has declared the beginning from the end and the end from the beginning! Sit back and watch My awesome revelations and manifestations unfold, declares God. Although the way has been long and narrow, I have sent forth Spirit to set the records straight. No matter what the circumstances and situations look like, simply shout **Hallelujah Anyhow**! Surely, my amazing grace has brought you thus far and grace shall lead you on.

This day marks the beginning of the _Jabez Miracle Zone_. Whatsoever my people ask, in My Name, I shall give them the desires of their hearts providing their hearts are right towards me and their intentions / motives are pure, declares God. For there is life in the blood and the power of Life and Death abide in the tongue. As my people, whom I have called according to My Name, worship me- the Lord thy God in spirit and in truth, the outpouring of overflow blessings shall abound on every side, declares God.

My precious people are to prepare themselves for Divine Connections, for they are now being processed for _Miracle Territory_. So, in all their ways, they are to acknowledge me and guard their hearts with diligence. WAIT FOR ME, proclaims God, as I perform my works in affairs of the heart at the proper time- decently and in Divine Order. Let not your hearts be troubled, for I have already set the wheels in motion to straighten out everything that seems awry. Therefore, because I AM God of more than enough, Supernatural Recompense and complete restoration is on the brink of fruition. Continue to pray without ceasing, holding fast to my word and promises for your lives, while the enemy of your soul is brought to utter ruin right before your very eyes. All broken things are fixed, wholeness, peace, and prosperity downpours across the land! As my people position themselves to serve as a blessing to others, I will bless them suddenly, immediately, and forever more, declares the Lord of Hosts. Finally, yet most importantly, the Highest Favor shall follow them wherever they go beginning right now, as My Spirit flows through them to reach out to others in need. I AM the Great I AM, your ever-present help at all times. Behold the magnificence of the One True Living God that abides with and within you forever more!

Amen

Tuesday Morning
30 September 2003 @ 0635 Hours

Glory and Grace is forever abounding-- expansive throughout Creation on this day, declares the Lord of Hosts. Surely, I say unto you that I- the Lord your God who is far greater than every circumstance and situation-- shall provide you with the Wisdom and Insights of that which was done in secret, a remarkable Inheritance of deeper strength and fortitude within seven days! Therefore, let not your hearts be troubled, for I have not given unto my people the spirit of fear, but that of Power, Love, and Stability of Mind. Be anxious for nothing, for should My people receive the manifestations before all is completely processed, then it shall not do you well. Be still and wait on me, for I can and will do these very things far more effectively and rapidly than one would ever be able to imagine! I also open doors that no person can close and close doors that those of ill intent have left opened, hoping to entrap you. Therefore, at all times, walk the High Road and step only over the thresholds of those doors that I have propped opened for you, says God. Should another attempt to walk through a door that was left open for my people, the door will slam, the burglar bars will drop down, and the lights will be turned off because they are illegally trespassing on territory that is not theirs.
(Moment of Meditation) ...

In order to walk through the open doors, preparation of the rarest kind will have taken place years before, while my people will have been thoroughly processed from the inside out. If the people of God are unprepared to inhabit the new territory, opportunity, and experiences, then they shall continue to be refined and instructed, to a greater degree until they have become more agile and discipled to inherit that which was promised as Supernatural Territories. Truly, I say unto you, proclaims God, *do not speak OF the mountains*, yet SPEAK TO THE MOUNTAINS with authority in who you are, coming into alignment with the Spirit Principles, thus shifting everything within your sphere of influence into proper order and positions! Haste makes waste!! So, in all things, being a faithful steward in the little things, opens the doorways of tremendous blessing, grace, and supernatural empowerment...

When the people are brought to a place where they are at the end of their own means and sufficiency, surely, they can put their hope, trust, and faith in God Almighty, believing that all things shall be provided for, even connections and opportunities. This is the time and now is the place, that I will promote and exalt those who are diligent and faithful, that they will know and understand it was not by might nor by power, but only through My Spirit that abides within them that has caused them to triumph, despite seasons of hardship and adversity. The way has been paved and the lines drawn in the sand-- where previous borders and limitations have been pushed back and territories have been broadened. Where the forces of darkness once set the boundary lines and dared my people to step across, declares God, the Kingdom of God has suffered violence, the violent and those violated have come to take everything back by force.
(Moment of Meditation)

As those who have been at battle begin to take stances of execution awaiting their next instruction / assignment prior to the attacks and frontal assaults, then the adversaries start to quiver, back down, draw up peace treaties, and return everything that was stolen from the people of God, thereby being **PAID IN FULL** *__of interest and escrow accounts__*. The opposition will even give from their own needs just to settle the disputes quickly so that they may make hasty departures and their lives will be preserved for such a time as this. The darkness comes to ruin and is slaughtered at the stake by the works of their own hands. Those cunning and cut-throats cannot be entrusted as to not come after my people again when their backs are turned, and their guards are down. Henceforth, they will not be allowed to rise again to positions of power for the sake of wreaking havoc in the lives of God's people.

Stand on the decrees and declarations that I have spoken to and within YOU, then shall you be shown great and mighty things suddenly and immediately. Let the chosen and committed vessels of the Highest God stand up to be counted and redeemed of all their transgressions and iniquities, says God. Let the words of thy mouth and meditation of thy hearts be pleasing and acceptable at all times, thus says the Lord God Almighty on this faithful day. Peace and Grace be unto All!!

Amen.

Wednesday Morning
01 October 2003 @ 0045 Hours

Hallelujah! Behold! This is the breaking forth of a brand-new day, declares the Lord of Hosts. Just because it is dark outside does not make it nonetheless morning time. *(Moment of Meditation)* ... Although the sun is yet to rise, the coming of the glorious daylight shall happen and everything will awaken at the brink of sunrise. Surely, even the flowers, trees, and grass know when the sun comes up. As the world displays its marvelous splendor of a new day, the Lord thy God breathes the breath of life for Divine Renewal and Restoration of the fruitful things that have lay dormant and unattended for so long. Because I am God and I neither sleep nor slumber, the minds and hearts of my people are being renewed and restored. The things that once lay on a solid foundation, but somehow fell through the cracks and seemingly shattered beyond mending, God Almighty- brings forth Healing, Wholeness, Health, and Prosperity to the land of those who strive to do what is right and operate in the precepts of Love. And in all things- prayer, supplication, praise, and thanksgiving shall forever be the tasks set forth for each day. Now is the time, that I put my people in places and situations that they must believe me at my word, or they will not receive what is promised without faith, diligence, and trust. There is no middle ground! Either you have faith in me, the Lord of Hosts for the things that look impossible, or you do not! Right- NOW FAITH is the substance of things hoped for and the evidence of things not yet seen.

No stone shall be left unturned. Therefore, I beseech you by way of Divine Mercies, Dearest Sons and Daughters of God Jehovah in the Highest, to remain steadfast in all that you do for your family and the community of believers in faith. If then, my people that I call by my name shall humble themselves in the midst of the adversity; I shall bring them out into Glory Abounding! Forever and ever, I am God in times of feast and famine. Shout Hallelujah for the dawning of a New Days and Favorable Seasons!

Amen

Thursday Morning
02 October 2003 @ 0920 Hours

Glory and Praise unto the Lord of Hosts at this very hour, for abiding as creator and sustainer of life, health, and posterity abounding. As I praise and worship Almighty God on this day, I shout Hallelujah! and rejoicing exuberantly because God is greater than all problems, circumstances, and situations. As surely as The Great I AM provided the ram in the bush for Abraham and made a way out of no way for Ruth, so shall all my needs be provided for!

Miraculous Interventions, outpouring of miracles, breakthroughs untold, and supernatural manifestations and favor are the hierarchal factors beginning this day that shall prove as signs and wonders of Jehovah God- the Author and Finisher of our Faith indeed. Verily, I say unto you on this day: "I AM God and do all things well. That which has been done before, I shall do it repeatedly, yet not in the same ways. There is no ending point to my forever-abounding provision and works, declares Jehovah Shalom, (Our God of Peace)." Take heed of my instructions and I shall impart unto you marvelous ideas, witty inventions, and innovative knowledge that produces great wealth as an inheritance. Those who have mocked, ridiculed, persecuted, slandered, maligned, gossiped, and slaughtered my chosen Sons and Daughters in spirit shall be dealt with severely. I shall raise up my people in the presence of their enemies and those that have condemned my people shall bear witness to the workings and favor of Almighty God in the lives of the remnant of God. The very ones that have laughed, scoffed, and ripped my people apart with their malicious tongues will be made to eat the bread of shame, confusion, and public humiliation, and then will be brought to a place of repentance unto the Lord of Hosts, while begging for forgiveness from those that they have spitefully abused and misused. *(Moment of Meditation)* ...

In this new season, my people shall reap the rewards of seeds planted long ago and paramount favor shall be the fruits of their harvests. There is no hiding place for they that have proven wayward and rebellious in spirit, as they have been unfaithful on all accords and in relationships. Truly, I say unto you, those who are faithful in the little that they have shall be blessed with much more! Those who have been unfaithful in the small things shall not receive great things until they have proven as wise and trusted stewards over the most miniscule gifts that I have placed into their hands and hearts, proclaims God Almighty.

Although my people have faced strife and insanity from every direction, declares God, I have sent forth the Holy Spirit to set the records straight and to vindicate those that were repeatedly wronged. I will give them gold for their grief and silver for their sorrows and shame. Rejoice, for I AM the Lord God Almighty and I have never seen the righteous forsaken or my faithful Sons and Daughters out begging for bread.

Previous circumstances and situations will dissipate at record speed and the adversaries will flee in order to spare their own lives. As jealously, hatred, greed, and envy, sent from the pits of darkness, has sought to devour my people, the Kingdom of God suffered violence, the violent and those violated shall take it all back by force! They shall bow down on their knees, pray without ceasing, offering sacrifices of praise and thanksgiving, and then bear witness to the wonders and miraculous works in the land of the living. Worry not! For those who had sown seeds of discord, disdain, disrespect, and dishonor, so shall they reap a harvest of those seeds that have been parceled out! Those who make a mockery of the downtrodden, surely shall they be demolished through the works of their own hands. *(Moment of Meditation)* ...

This marks the territorial barriers that shall block out all hindering spirits and strongholds of darkness from the

Promised Land. Rejoice! Those who steal the joy of others are sowing seeds of death unto themselves. I AM the Lord God Almighty and the records are being set straight.
Amen

Friday Morning
03 October 2003 @ 0600 Hours

Great and merciful Almighty Divine, Exalted is thy Name, thy Kingdom come in earth as it is in the realm of the Cosmos of All Creation. Give us this day our daily bread as we give you thanksgiving and praise. Lead us not into temptation but deliver us from evil. Forgive us this day our debts and frailties of faithfulness, as we forgive our debtors and transgressors. For yours, oh Lord is the Kingdom of Glory and let your will be done for our lives in spite of us and our iniquities and shortcomings. Great and mighty are you, oh Lord, for you have declared the beginning from the end and the end from the beginning. I am available to and for you to use on this day, that I may be a blessing to those that set their faces towards you. Allow me to look neither to the left or right, but only to you whom is my help, strength, shelter, provider, and kinsman redeemer. It is the Lord my God that heals me and restores my mind to perfect peace. Regardless of circumstances or situations, you are still God and there is none like you. The way has already been made for seemingly impossible situations to be resolved! Shout Hallelujah unto the God Almighty!

"Behold! exclaims the Lord of Hosts. Newness and renewal of mind, body, spirit, emotions, and finances are hereby in effect. As my people praise me today, they shall watch and bear witness to the shackles being broken, and the captives set free from the traps of the destruction. Bask in my goodness and glory, proclaims Almighty God, while keeping your tongue from uttering idle words, and I shall hand over to you the harvests abounding and your loved ones that you have fasted, prayed, and interceded for. They shall be hand-delivered bearing fruit and gifts. Although they know not what they ought to do, I am God and I have led them in the presence of my Sons and Daughters in Truth and Love, with a spirit of forgiveness, repentance, humility, and

reconciliation. They are to be received with grace and mercy. Although they are not where they should be in me, I am working this masterpiece from the inside out and the finished product has not yet been unveiled, for it is a work incomplete. However, pray without ceasing and speak to the future in the spirits of the people and not to their natural / physical being. I shall reward my people in great measure for their faithfulness and follow-through to adhere to my instructions and guidance. Surely, if a person is constantly reminded and slaughtered by his / her past, they shall always be in regression instead of pressing towards the mark for the higher calling in Spirit of reconciliation.
(Moment of Meditation) ...

Listen carefully with discerning ears and be not hard hearted, but diligently guard your heart because these matters are of a delicate and fragile nature. Receive my people as you would receive your own children if they strayed off the path of clear thinking, then humbly asked to come back home and into my grace that abides within you. I am God and I have imparted into my people who worship me in spirit and truth, the spirit of reconciliation and unconditional love. Although my precious Sons and Daughters struggle with anger, rejection, hurt, strife, discord, and vengeful thoughts, they are to be not swept up in the ways of this world but be transformed by the renewing of their minds through Spirit of the Living God. They are to give all these things over to me, the Lord Almighty, and I shall heal my people everywhere they hurt, providing they once again nurse the wounded ones back to life and in the ways of love and wholeness. My people, who I call by My Name are to continue to display the mind and ways of Love that I have so graciously poured into them. Yet, there are so many that have never before experienced the love, compassion, and virtue of God through my people. I, the Lord God Almighty shall repay whatever debts my people owe, providing they hand all of their issues over to me. Stand still and know that I am God. I require my mature Sons and

Daughters to always the walk the high road, no matter how badly they desire to act out and step into the lower levels of primal existence. However, should they trust me in the ways that I am leading them; they shall not be put to shame. Then I, the Lord thy God, shall rebuild and restore, stripping out everything that is unlike Me-- in those who are wholeheartedly devoted to Me in all their ways. The finished product will result in foundational truth and intimate fellowship that was built on, and within Me- *Jehovah Shalom-* (The God of Peace.)

As for the adversaries that have chosen to come against that which I have ordained in my peoples' lives, they have subjected themselves to becoming the living dead, wallowing in the ashes of destruction created by their own misdeeds. Henceforth, those enemies shall not torment my people ever again. I have bestowed blessings of faith and will heal, restore, and renew all breaks and cracks within Divine Covenant Partnerships, declares God Almighty. Speak life into the once flourishing trees, says God, and I shall resurrect, reconstruct, and reestablish covenants in fortitude and resistance to all attacks and deceptions of the opposing forces. *(Moment of Meditation)* ...

Believe me at my word, declares God. Although you are hesitant and adamant about this entire situation, believe in me, the Lord of Hosts, and place your trust only in me and I shall not abandon you, but shall make all barren things fruitful. Trust in me, God of your Soul, as I will teach my people how-to walk-in freedom. Let my will be done in the lives of my said people for my Kingdom purposes, and I will not allow you to eat the bread of shame. Stand in faith and expectation of manifestations coming forth in that which has been promised by the Forever Faithful God. Rejoice, for the time is NOW!

Amen

Saturday Afternoon
04 October 2003 @ 1230 Hours

Glory, Grace, and Mercy abounds as the Spirit of Almighty God rests and abides in this place at this very hour. God has said that whatever we ask for in faith with His purposes in the forefront, he will give unto us in great measure. Truly, I say unto you, as surely as I have provided for you before, I will do it repeatedly and my provisions never run out or become extinct, declares God Almighty.

This is a day of changed focus, declares God. They that have been distracted and dissuaded from those things that I have called and purposed for them to do within the Kingdom of God are now being sanctioned and summonsed by the Spirit of Truth from within, that they may come into alignment and Divine Order is established in their lives! Everything that was previously out of order, proclaims God, shall now be thrusted with the force of a volcanic eruption for succinct alignment. As my peoples' footsteps shall be ordered, guided, and directed by me every step of the way, I shall pave the road less traveled that the Higher Ground may be seized and secured. As in a waltz, first one must be led by the headship or leader in order to learn and anticipate the moves carefully, then after the steps have been closely monitored and adhered to, there is no longer the need to watch one's feet. The moves shall come naturally as a second nature / instinct so that confidence is built up, then a vibrant flow of the Grace and Empowerment shall catapult you in the myriad of twists and turns to avoid the traps, while crushing the head of ill-intentions! Shout with voices of triumph and praise because I, the Lord thy God have sent forth the angels to encamp around the predestined families of God and no weapon formed against them shall prosper. Surely, I am God Most High, and far greater than every circumstance and situation that anyone could possibly encounter. Have faith in the God Almighty of Creation, who is a prayer-answering, miracle-working, loved one delivering God that demolishes every imposed or perceived limitation. I shall show you my hands of favorable dispensation because it is my presence that you have sought.

The harvests are bountiful and the laborers, so I implore my people to dare not sit idly by and wait to reap harvests of those things for which they have not sown seed. I- the Lord Forever Faithful provides seed to the Sowers and bread unto those that feed my sheep. My people are hereby forewarned that they should not be found guilty of owning a bakery and not sparing a loaf of bread to brothers and sisters in need of food for their families. *(Moment of Meditation)* ... In all things, declares God, my people are to acknowledge me in all of their ways and affairs, from the smallest task to the greatest projects. My people are to be diligent in all their affairs and remain steadfast in prayer because I, the Lord thy God, shall bless those that are faithful, from the least to the greatest.

Distress not over these circumstances and situations because I am turning all things around and causing them to work in the favor of my people, for I am the Lord of Hosts. Promotions, Divine Visitations, Supernatural Favor, and Supernatural Appointments are on the brink of fruition right now. So, be on point and stand alert for abounding glory, as families shall be completely restored in less than fourteen days, declares God. Watch me, the Lord of Hosts perform quick works while setting the captives free.

Amen!

Sunday Morning
05 October 2003 @ 0730 Hours

Hallelujah! As we are called to worship the Lord thy God in spirit and in truth on this day, there is a quickening of the Holy Ghost that shall be loosed with fervency and a sense of urgency pouring forth to set the captives free, proclaims God Almighty. Surely, the race is not given to the swift, or the battles to the strong, but to they who have endured until the end, while fighting the good fight of faith through prayer and supplication. *(Moment of Meditation)* ...

The time has come for all commitments that were previously broken to be restored in good faith and Godly character. Behold! I am the Lord God Almighty and I have no interest in the comforts of my people, but in the condition of their hearts and the countenance of their character and integrity. Truly, I say unto you, all people that have wavered in commitments, tarnished covenants, and faltered in the partnerships that I have placed them in, are being called out loudly to come into right standing and take responsibility for the infringements upon those whom they have wronged. Be not dismayed, for I have sent forth a wave of peace to make amends and bring forth recompense for all that was not done decently and in Divine Order. Get ready, proclaims God, for the time has arrived and the places have been marked for Divine Order to be steadfastly confirmed and reestablished. All those that have thrown their houses, lives, and families into disarray and discord are being sanctioned to reconcile with the spirit of humility, grace, forgiveness, and total repentance. The ministry of reconciliation becomes possible where Love is at the forefront and pride takes a backseat. Therefore, be not accused of receiving the instructions yet allowing it to fall upon deaf ears. Many are the afflictions of the righteous, but the Lord God almighty delivers from them all. May the grace and mercy of God bring forth healing and

restoration, as the power of Love sets the captives free. In all things and through all seasons, be of good courage, sound mind, and a merry heart, for a merry heart breaks down the roots of contention, strife, and bitterness.
(Moment of Meditation)

Offer up reasonable and acceptable sacrifices of praise, worship, and thanksgiving because as faithful Sons and Daughters of the Almighty God, the people are required to produce and reproduce the fruits of faith, hope, and love. Yet, the greatest of all these is Love. Where there is no love, hope vacates and faith dissipates, declares the Lord of Hosts. Walk not by faith, or by sight, and lean not to thy own understanding. The vision is yet for an appointed time and the appointed time is about to arrive. Suit up in the full armor of God and in having done all that one can do, abide in faith and faithfulness, never failing to give thanks unto the Lord of Hosts at all times whether feasting or in lands of famine. In the seasons of storm, remain steadfast in prayer. The foundations that were built upon the rock-solid relationship with the Lord thy God shall not crumble into the sea, nor blow away with the passing winds, proclaims God Almighty. Do not be distracted by what is seen, for surely everything that is now seen is subject to change. There is hereby a change in the season, a shift in the heavens, a flood of the Divine Empowerment, and earthquakes that birth manifestations…

Walk not in the counsel of the foolish, but in all things, acknowledge God in all of your ways. Waste not and want never! I am your provider, and all needs are met without fail. Grace, grace, abounding grace shall overrun you and gratitude shall be the orchard that you harvest from, says God.

Broken focus must not be!!! For everything that has been stolen and destroyed in the lives of those that worship God in spirit and in truth, it shall be poured back into their lives exponentially and multi-dimensional. Love, favor, peace, wholeness, prosperity, covenant relationships, and fresh inspiration shall seek out the pure at heart. The exiled and confused will return as the Spirit of God from within has grieved them about the mistreatment and negligence of relationship with the prophets of God. Give no care or particular thought to this or any other matter, for the angels are encamped around families of love who hold my purposes in the forefront. Those dwelling places and covenant partners of the Lord of Hosts shall not be overtaken by death, harm, or destruction. In all things, regardless of what circumstances of situations dictate, I alone am still the Lord God Almighty and I have never seen those in right standing with me forsaken or my faithful, humble Sons and Daughters our begging for bread. I am the Lord of Hosts...I am not a man that I should lie, neither the son of man that I should repent. Whatsoever I have decreed, it is so, in overflowing capacity!

Arise! Even the angels rejoice because the victory has been won. I am the Lord of Hosts and I have emphatically stated, "Touch not my anointed ones and do my prophets no harm. Whatever has been done to the least of them has also been done unto me- God Almighty. No person shall declare war upon those who are faithful and devoted to Almighty and expect to be successful and fruitful. The promises of God are always yes and amen!

I have given unto my people of purpose, Godly character, and purity of heart, the power to tread upon the heads of the serpents while snapping their fingers at the vipers and vultures causing them to flee swiftly. This is no laughing matter! For they who have laughed and mocked my chosen ones, shall be dealt with in the same manner which they have served. Immediately after the smoke clears, all laughter will have ceased because the oppressors will be lain to rest for the dead to bury its own, proclaims God.

Let this be a day of rejoicing and celebration. Let the glory, favor, and honor of the Lord thy God rise among us! The dead can tell no lies or properly disburse wealth. Surely, the wealth of those unjust and unscrupulous shall be reallocated to those who seek to do good throughout humanity, whereas the darkness shall not prevail. In all of thy quests, ask for Wisdom and seek to receive Understanding!

Amen

Monday Morning
06 October 2003 @ 0615 Hours

Praise unto God Almighty, who has declared the beginning from the end and the end from the beginning. On this day, you are visited with recompense for all of the hurts endured, accompanied by clarity, stability and peace of mind, body, and spirit that shall overpower all the shadows of darkness, proclaims God. As I have set forth the vision and path for the lives of my precious people, although many feel as if they have missed the mark for my higher calling, I will provide with great measure the Wisdom as an inheritance. Be not deceived or confused by all that you have seen, including the smoke screens and mirrors because I- the Lord of Hosts, have set the course and you shall go forth in my name as my appointed ambassador. Therefore, praise me even more and thank me for the consecration processes. My will is to strip everything out of you that hinders you from My Absolute Best for your life. I have not given unto you the spirit of fear, but of power, love, and a stability mind. So, rest and abide in me, stand on my word and revelation knowledge that has been imparted—trusting that all these things are working together for your good unbelievably. It is decreed that you are the head and not the tail, above and not beneath, the lender and not the borrower. Furthermore, death, harm, or destruction shall not overtake you, proclaims God!

The attacks have come at you from every side, and when the force of darkness attempts to demolish my chosen ones where they live. However, those who set out to create havoc in the lives of others set themselves up to be mangled. No drop of a prophet's blood shall be shed by the enemy unless it is in conjunction to Higher Purpose. Therefore, assaults on my hand select shall render the attackers as the living dead. I am the Lord of Hosts and the rock upon which you stand!

Those who sow seeds of discord among fellow brothers and sisters, and within families creating strife and dissention, are worse than unbelievers, declares God. When there is bloodshed on a person's hands, the blood of the righteous Sons and Daughters of God cry out unto me, for the blood is the lifeline of my people. When attacked, simply lift up your hands and know that I shall send forth the angels to encamp around you. Rest and abide in me because I am the Lord of Hosts and I neither sleep nor slumber. I see all, hear all, and know all. Those who put their hope and trust in Almighty Creator shall live by faith in God and the gates of darkness shall never prevail!

Shout Hallelujah! For the Glory of the Lord God Almighty serves as your constant strength, help, health, source, and protection. Now, let there be rejoicing throughout the earth, for the Lord Almighty is worthy to be praised every moment of every day.

Amen

Wednesday Morning
08 October 2003 @ 1105 Hours

Glory Hallelujah! The battle is finished, and the war has been won, declares God Almighty. As surely as you have hearkened unto my presence on this day, all shall be well with you. Though the anguish and torment come to steal, kill, deceive, and destroy, I have sent forth the Holy Spirit to set the captives free. Regardless of what the circumstances and situations look like, I am still God, and every assignment of darkness has been put to death and brought to a screeching halt. In such an hour as this, those of hateful countenance come forth with full force to deceive my people into believing that they are not loved and treasured of God. However, the spirit of darkness propagates lies, whereas I am the Lord of Hosts who has ordained you for such a time as this. Therefore, look neither to the left or right but keep your eyes focused on me that you will not get distracted and led into destruction.

Unto mine people who worship me in Spirit and in Truth, I am Creator and Sustainer. So, I know what my people are capable of, and their behaviors come as no surprise to me, for I know all things. I have consecrated my precious Sons and Daughters whom I have approved as faithful. Yet, there is much more work to be done so that they may be purified in demeanor, in speech, in etiquette, and in all actions, thoughts, and reactions, declares God. I am the Lord of Hosts and I have not given my people the spirit of fear, but of power, love, and a satiety mind. In all mine peoples' ways, they are to acknowledge me, the Lord thy God. When they find that they have gotten out of alignment with the origin of the Creation, they are to wholly forgive themselves, while coming unto Me- The Almighty unashamedly and I shall wash them clean and wipe out the transgression from their minds. No matter what has happened, I shall turn these messes into powerful messages that shall confound the worldly wise, enlighten and empower the ignorant, and set the bound free indeed. The called and chosen shall live by faith in God and the gates of destruction shall not prevail.

Be not deceived, dear people, Love is the answer to many sorrows. Those who are downtrodden are called to ARISE! I require them to get back up again and drink of the living waters so that they are replenished, where death, harm, or destruction shall not prevail over them, says God Almighty. If for any reason I stop my people in the midst of their routines so that they may go to help one of my children by way of prayer and intercession, to promote the betterment and wellbeing of others, then I shall also reward their faithfulness quickly, immediately, supernaturally, and abundantly. Wherever there is a shortage, there is also an abundant supply in the vicinity. I am obligated to send forth provisions to care for my people and their families because the prophets are subject to my every disposal at every hour of every day. For unto those that have proven faithful to step outside their personal habitat / comfort zone to minister to just one, without agenda, motive, or for the purposes of being seen, then they have proven trustworthy to minister to millions. Despise not the small beginnings, declares God, for I raise up those that are diligent and obedient to mine work.

Now and forever more, be not perplexed over that which I have already declared is done. When having done all that I have required and all that you know how, just stand and watch me perform signs and wonders on your behalf. Though the kingdom of God suffers violence, the violent and violated shall take it all back by force, not by physical means, but through fervent prayer and supplication. Do not doubt that which I have imparted into thee and allow not the mockery and ramblings of others to tarnish your good name or Godly character. Before they breathe their last breath, they will acknowledge that they have been brought to the place of darkness by the words of their own lips and attacks they have launched against mine hand select priests and priestesses of Almighty God. Be ever watchful, pay close attention, and listen with discerning ears, for my promises are steadfast!

Cherish and savor each word that I impart into you, as I shall enlighten you further of all the hidden things that are to come and is past. Behold! The salvation of the Lord is your strength. In all things, exercise patience and restraint, for the wicked comes about to tempt thee into acting out of the flesh instead of flowing in the Spirit Truth. I am the Lord your God and have declared the end from the beginning and the beginning from the end. So, be not mistaken, misled, or dissuaded by the opinions of others. I am the Lord of Hosts and have predestined you for glory, grace, favor, and honor. Therefore, you will never be made to eat the bread of shame or humiliation in the midst of your adversaries. I shall do all that I have said and even more because the joy of the Lord is your strength. These are your words of revelation knowledge on this day, says God, and I will prove myself faithful on every accord. Rejoice! Anticipate Divine Appointments, Visitations, and / or phone calls on this day. While in wait, rejoice in advance over the manifestations that are yet to be revealed.

Amen

Thursday Evening
09 October 2003 @ 1625 Hours

Rejoice! For great and mighty are the wonderful works of the Lord Almighty indeed! When the precious people, whom I call by my name, declares the Lord of Hosts—come into my presence within the altar of their hearts, worshiping me in Spirit and Truth, then surely, I will heed their cries and inhabit their praises. Although they may not know what to ask for or exactly what they have need of, the abiding Spirit makes way through fervent prayer and intercession to set the captives free, while putting every assignment of darkness to flight, proclaims God. Blessed are those who bear the burdens and pains of fellow sisters and brothers, empowering others to do good, well, better, and excel in every arena of livelihood. Truly, I say unto my people, I am the One True Living God, which has sent dispatched the angels and every provision so that my children shall not dwell in lack. In essence, should they lose their way, then they are to always keep at the forefront of remembrance that I AM the Lord of Creation. I am the way, the truth, and the life / light and nothing shall separate you from the love of God. I have ways of leading every person to the place that they should be. Providing they are willing, it is less painful than continuing in the ways that lead to self-destruction, proclaims God.

Blessed is the name of the Lord God forever more; magnificent are works of the Great I AM—Forever Faithful and true indeed. Brace yourselves, for those that worship me in spirit and in truth, shall be eyewitnesses to fabulous, miraculous wonders of God Almighty in this upcoming month. Surely, because I have done it before, I will do it again, but not necessarily in the same way. I have declared the beginning from the end and the end from the beginning. Be still and know that I am God; I have worked out all of the intricate details to the point that my peoples' resistance and stress is not required. The one paramount requirement of my people is their FAITH in me. Faith is the substance of things hoped for, and the evidence of things not seen. Just because something is not seen, declares God, does not mean that it does not exist. *(Moment of Meditation)* ... It may be neatly tucked away and strategically hidden for an appointed time, so that all things may be brought into perfected alignment before the unveiling of the gifts. If my people believe that I AM God of Creation and Caretaker of their souls, the giver of every good and perfect gift, knowing with steadfast conviction that as surely as I have decreed a thing, so shall it be unto them! Although there may not be clear understanding at first, for one is not privy to all the steps that I have administered to bring this thing to pass, they are to trust wholeheartedly that I am God!

In the land of exiles and barren plots, I have set my steadfastly committed people of purpose apart from all others so that I may retain their undivided attention. Although they maybe experiencing seasons of what feels like famine right now, it does not mean that the Lord God Almighty have abandoned them or left them to die. It simply means that my people are to trust me unconditionally and know that the way has already been paved for them to receive exactly what is needed for the place that they are in. The hard places do not determine my love, like, or dislike for my children. They must learn to praise and worship me whether they are in dungeons of abasement, as well as in high places of pristine nobility. However, because I alone am the Omnipotent Jehovah God, my people are to honor me in who they were created to be, for I have spared them of other trials and tribulations that would be too much for them to bear. *(Moment of Meditation)* ... Not all of my children suffer the same trials because not all are equipped to handle the same adversity and afflictions, declares God. To whom much is given, much more is required. And unto they whom much is required of, much more shall be generously given. Take note of all blessings great and small because as quickly as one has abundance and no lack, while yet another dwells in poverty and afflictions on every side, the tables can turn at the drop of a leaf from a tree in autumn. The trials and tests have been sent to strengthen my people and build their character. Take heart and be of good courage, understanding that the battle is not yours, it is mine, thus says the Lord of Hosts. So, stop fighting and wrestling with the processes and rest and abide in me, flowing in the Spirit of Truth, Peace, and Wholeness. I am the Lord God Almighty and I attend the cares and needs of my people.

I am the Lord thy God. I have called my people of truth into Divine Purpose, Kingdom Vision, and Supernatural Provision. As they walk in my purposes, grasping a firm revelation, and readjust their sights on the vision that I have ordained from their lives, they shall receive the provisions that I shall send forth to bring the works to completion. Rejoice in the renewal, restoration, and refreshing, for the vision was dampened and your minds suffered attacks, yet I AM a God of total healing and rejuvenation. Hallelujah, Hallelujah, Hallelujah!

Grace abounds, declares the Lord of Hosts. I have given the visions, so clap your hands and sing new songs of joy, then bear witness to the manifested signs, wonders, and miracles right before your very eyes. Expect the unexpected as all things are made clear. Divine Interventions, communications, and covenant connections are at the forefront.

Amen

Saturday Morning
11 October 2003 @ 0410 Hours

Praise unto the God Most High for great awakenings! On this day, says God Almighty, I shall show myself faithful in all that I have decreed within the past thirty days, and you- dear child, shall bear witness to the declarations, decrees, and promises without fail. Prepare for visitors, for what I have given unto you is rich fruit of the spirit and sustaining character that has carried you through struggles, storms, madness, famine, and remarkable feats that defy unprecedented odds. Through your workings of faith and faithfulness to what I have called you to do that I, the Lord of Hosts move mightily in your situations and circumstances. Regardless of what was before-- this does not determine the outcomes for what shall be in the NOW! Yet, in all things, I am still God! The naysayers and all-purpose busybodies shall not receive the satisfaction of gloating over your apparent downfall because the perceived downfall is but an allusion that causes them to sit in a comfort zone as they let down their guards. *(Moment of Meditation)* ... Just as they begin to celebrate and rejoice over your situation, they arrogantly believe they have been victorious in their attacks, says God. However, the Spirit of God that abides within you shall raise you up from the pits, place your feet on solid ground, stabilize you in supernatural grace, then catapult you into a greater dimension. Therefore, steady yourself to reap an inheritance for all your hardships, tears, and humiliation. For truly I say unto you—those who place their faith in me- the Eternal Everlasting God, the assignments of darkness shall never prevail over you!!

At this very hour, proclaims God, those who have wronged you are toiling with no rest from their weariness. Because you have been in my presence as the much of the world has slept and rested, blessed, and highly favored are you in this very present moment! Now is the appointed time that brings about restitution, retribution, and recompense, righting all wrongs being done to My people by those that have inflicted ill-will unto they who have proven faithful unto God.

Be not dismayed by where you are because I have already declared the beginning from the end and the end from the beginning. Cast not your pearls out to swine, for they shall trample on precious jewels and priceless treasures, for the swine only has appreciation for wallowing in mud and feasting in gluttony. It is completely unnecessary for my people to wear flashing neon signs around their necks to show the world who they belong to. I- the Lord of Hosts, have imparted the light within so bright until most onlookers will need to wear shades / eye protection when they gaze upon my people of purpose in radiating brilliance and impeccable character.

Let the joy of the Lord thy God serve as your strength each day. Expect the unexpected, says God, for the unexpected is far more spectacular than even you could ever imagine! Blessed and Highly Favored are you, for whatsoever my people have set their hands to do in honor and spirit commitment unto Me, the Lord of Hosts, and through my instruction and direction / guidance, it shall not return void. Do not become weary in well doing for harvests are being released at the appointed time. As Thanksgiving Day is to be observed every day for those that awake in the land of the living, My people are to pray without ceasing, and those that have been gifted by charge of holy servitude to pray for others, they are to intercede for all people, places, and situations that innermost Wisdom brings to the forefront of their minds so that all things are rectified and surrendered unto the Kingdom of God.

Be not disillusioned by what is seen, because everything that is seen is subject to change, suddenly and immediately. Expect nor accept mere apologies, but true, genuine, and sincere repentance notions.

My people that worship me in spirit and in truth shall receive all that they have a heart for, regardless of the opinions of others. I am God, and I will do exactly as I have said. Hold tight, for the blast off to the greater dimensions of insight and higher ground is in the works! Render unto Me, the Lord God Almighty, all Honor, Worship, Praise, and Thanksgiving, for I am the One True Living God forevermore!
Amen.

Sunday Morning
12 October 2003 @ 0320 Hours

Praises unto God Almighty, the keeper of my soul. You are the lover of my soul, comforter, friend, shelter, hope, redeemer. On this day, proclaims God Almighty, I shall visit you right where you live because you have been faithful to do my work at the slightest prompting of Spirit. Therefore, be of a merry and cheerful heart, for I shall bless thee in abundant measure for all diligence, says God Almighty. Even as you simply go about your routine, being a good steward over what I have blessed you with, the miracles and manifestations are about to overrun you, declares the Lord of Hosts. Therefore, this is the preparation period for you to be displayed as one who is called to uncommon action and service to humanity. Many wish to remain incognito, yet I shall perform great and mighty works through them, for they have shown me that they are willing, available, and take heed to the Divine Calling. For the gifts and callings of the Lord Jehovah God are irrevocable!

The visions have been amplified, and the revelations illuminated. Therefore, I am working on and through my set people so that **Divine Will**, precedence, and purposes are brought to fruition, proclaims the Lord of Hosts. Lift up your voice in triumph, because the victory has been won and the war is over.

On this day, proclaims God, you shall know that I have opened my hands to you as provisions, favor, blessings, miracles, and breakthroughs seek you out. Show mercy and compassion for the works that I am performing and know that I will not allow the work to remain incomplete, says God. Rest assured that I am a Father of Forgiveness and Agape Love unconditional. So, my people are to trust me as I minister unto their spirits as to how they are to conduct themselves, while extending grace to impart into the pains and sorrowful hearts of others, says God. There is no glory in being right, but grace and mercy in being in right standing with the God of your soul, for love covers a multitude of wrongdoing.

Literary works shall be made fruitful quickly, says God. My people suffer from lack of revelation knowledge. Let not my people remain ill informed, misinformed, or abide in ignorance due to lack of understanding, says God. Open thy hearts, hands, minds, and ears to Divine Connections, for they have not been placed in the pathways of my people by accident. Be slow to speak, yet careful to listen to what is being conveyed, which keeps one from making snap judgement calls.

No matter what it looks like, says God, family restoration and financial abundance is about to invade the worlds of my people that honor, revere, and acknowledge me in all of their ways, while doing what is right and just by others as well. So, let your mind be healed, as your joy, peace, and hope is renewed. For it is not by might, nor by power, but by and through the workings of Spirit that the captives are set free. Be not conformed by the ways of this world yet be transformed through the renewing of the mind. This marks the beginning of the supernatural outpouring of greater works in Me, says God.

Amen

Sunday Evening
12 October 2003 @ 1605 Hours

Praises unto the Lord God on High, for the presence of
Spirit establishes and confirms the indelible truth on the
mantles of our hearts. Therefore, no matter what has
happened, you shall still go forth and prosper because no
force of darkness is unable to nullify My word, proclaims
God. The deal and covenant that I have made with my
remnant still stands, regardless of what has been said about
my people or done to them. For I have decreed that you
shall live, thrive, prosper, be in good health and wholeness,
even as your soul prospers! This day marks the beginning of
Divine Impartations that shall shake the locales, then the
nations, proclaims God. It is because I have gifted and
equipped some with the fruit of true intercession. Prayer is
the gift that keeps on giving! In all your ways, declares the
Lord of Hosts, acknowledge me, and then you shall not fail in
any task that I have assigned. No matter what has been done
and said to and about my people, I will bless them in all their
comings and goings, despite the evil tidings of the wicked.
So, be not dismayed over those who have slandered you and
broken trust and faith with you. Because I am God, I always
have the last word!

As you praise and worship me in spirit and in truth, I shall
bless your every pure thought. Every pure and fruitful
thought that enters the minds of my set people, I shall bless
and create the manifestation. Be not weary in well doing, for
your harvests are about to be hand-delivered with interests
and penalties in spite of previous delays! Carefully discern
what others say to you, whereas, they have not the insight for
the vision that I have imparted into thee. Surely, they may
know me, yet they shirk my calling in their own lives because
they do not want to walk the road of righteousness nor do
what I have required of them. They only desire to do what is
convenient for them! In essence, says God, they would like

to forget those places from where I have delivered them. So, be on guard, dear child. Truly, I say unto thee, all will know that I am the Lord your God and have sent forth the angels to set the records straight for you --while the Holy Spirit smooths out all the crooked places, thus blazing new trails as I have empowered you to be a trailblazer and pathfinder. Pick up your crosses and follow me, declares the Lord of Hosts, and grace untold shall be yours each and every day, for mine grace and mercy are more than sufficient for those whom honor the Lord God in Spirit and in Truth.

Although the way appears dim now, please know and understand that I, the Lord thy God have placed a few select others with and around you to pick you up when you fall and fan the flame when the fire threatens to go out. Therefore, precious people of God, rest when you are tired and refuel when you are weary in well doing so that you will not wear thin, and your health remains optimal and strong for taking on future days. Before feeding others, feed yourselves first, for if you are running on empty, you will not have the strength to pour into others as I direct and instruct you to do, say God. Just know that your steps are ordered, guided, and directed by God Almighty. *(Moment of Meditation)* ...

Do not lose heart, the visitors will still come and will come with hearts of love and appreciation for your very lives, for you are rich in virtue, character, and strength. Even the strong Sons and Daughters of God require replenishment, restoration, and prayer after climbing out of the pits of vipers. At the same measures that I have forgiven, you are to forgive and feed others if they hunger and thirst after my spirit. I, the Lord thy God shall reward you bountifully for your graciousness. Do these things because I have done no less for you, and you are called to serve as mine hands extended. I am the Lord God Almighty and I am the way, the truth, and the light. So, let everything that have breath praise ye' the Lord of Hosts.
Amen

Monday Morning
13 October 2003 @ 1135 Hours

Glory unto the Lord of Hosts, for on this day, there is an outpouring of Grace in Spirit that shall flood God's people-- infiltrating the gates and assignments to overthrow the influences of the kingdom of darkness, says the Lord. There is no hiding place-- and no rock or stone shall be left unturned. They that have thrown rocks and hidden their hands shall be exposed. Those that have kept their hands to the plow, their eyes towards the higher calling in Spirit Consciousness, and their hearts in proper alignment shall be rewarded bountifully. Many may misinterpret and wrongly perceive my people in the natural, while they are called to the business of searching out the well springs of their own soul. For in the natural form, and to the naked eyes, souls of the reprobate do not bring forth excellent fruit. However, when one presses into God and worships Me in spirit and in truth, those who diligently seek to walk the high roads less traveled are destined for greatness as he / she adheres to my guidance and instruction, declares the Lord of Hosts.

Any tree that does not bear good fruit in its proper season is to be chopped down and cast into the fire. Yet, because I am a God of opportunities, I grant people the time and chances to turn from their vile ways that they might come to know me intimately and their lives be changed for the betterment and benefit of humanity. *(Moment of Meditation)* ...

Fellow humanity listens to what is said, however are to watch more carefully as to what is done in and out of darkness. For whatsoever lies in the hearts of a person shall surely surface eventually, whether they be good, bad, ugly, or indifferent, says God. In all things, the people who claim to know me are to allow their yes to be yes and their no's to stand as a firm no, for a double-minded person is unstable in all of his / her ways and shall not expect to receive anything from me, the Lord God Almighty over the great and the small. A person is only as stable as his/ her words, says God. Therefore, allow your hearing and listening to be in abundance, but may your speech be guarded carefully that idle words do not depart from the heart and mouth to defile others or themselves.

Be still and know that I am God, creating ways, means, and provision for you that is not readily conceivable this time. Provision comes forth out of what appears to be dead ends. Therefore, doubt not, simply trust and believe, having faith in the Lord your God who is Faithful and True.

As I have poured out my spirit, you have taken in more than the average vessel can hold, while imparting into others much of what I have given unto you. Arise! The joy of God is your strength indeed. So, do not grow tired in doing the right thing simply because it is right, for you shall reap millions-fold, multi-dimensional harvests in due season. You are on the brink of miracles and manifestations. So, be not only hearers of the word but listeners to the word, then doers of the word, and making a conscious choice of abiding in the ever-flowing spirit of God, flourishing in every good work to impart nourishment and sustenance of others. Conduct yourselves accordingly as outlined and governed spirit consciousness—alive and well within your soul so that blessings are not delayed. Offer up sacrifices of praise and phenomenal thanksgiving unto God Most High—for the greatest of all gifts is Love, Peace, and Gratitude.

Amen

Tuesday Morning
14 October 2003 @ 0615 Hours

Hallelujah! Honor, Gratitude, and Praise unto the Almighty, for surely the God of Recompense, Salvation and Deliverance reigns supreme. On this day, declares God Almighty, I shall pour out droves of grace and healing- drenched in uncommon favor, great works, and promises that shall not return unto you void. Regardless of what happened before, this is a new day and season. I have restored, repaired, and made anew all things that were previously of fruitful beginnings, to again flourish and thrive. This is a day of regeneration, declares the Lord God Almighty. Therefore, be not dismayed by what the situation looks like because everything that can be seen is subject to change quickly- even in the blink of an eye. So, do not be fooled by the smoke screens and mirrors, for these serve as tools of delusion, sent by the shadows of darkness to create distractions. Because I am God, stand solidly upon that which has been imparted into you and trust that what has been decreed over your life, regardless of what others think or say. I -the Lord of Hosts have given you the vision of things that shall happen. So, those who attempt to dissuade and discourage you from believing me at my never-failing word, simply pray for them, for the time shall arrive when they too shall bear witness to what will come to the fullness of fruition in your life. My word supersedes all opinions, doctrines, ideologies, and idiosyncrasies of humanity.

Stand on my word and be of sound faith, faithfulness, and courage, proclaims God Almighty. For those who put their full trust and confidence in me, while adhering to the instructions and guidance given by way of Spirit, they shall not be brought to shame or ruin! Therefore, ARISE in your calling, trusting that you have not been brought to this place to be abandoned by the Lord Almighty! The seeds that you

66

have sown are not in vain yet shall produce and reproduce bountiful harvests for generations to come!!

Amen

Tuesday Evening
14 October 2003 @ 1830 Hours

Glory and Grace unto the Lord of Hosts, for mighty are the works of The Great Divine indeed. As this day has sunk into evening and the evening soon dissipates into night, I – God Almighty shall do an unthinkable and unspeakable wonder on your behalf. Even though many have been denied this particular provision and favor, I shall make the way smooth for you to receive the manifestation because you have sought my face, not my hand, that I may impart into you wisdom of Divine Things. The vision is yet for an appointed time and the appointed time is rapidly approaching. In all things, give praise, thanks, and honor to the Lord thy God for all that you have need of, every provision is being released, creating miracles and manifestations right where you abide. Do not grow faint in doing well unto others, for surely you shall reap the harvests that I, the Lord thy God have promised. However, do not give up!!

Rejoice, precious people, for the crossings of the finished lines are close and the victory shall be handed over to those who have been faithful unto me, the Lord God Almighty. Give glory, grace, and honor unto the Lord of Hosts because I shall do all that I have said. Every provision needed shall be handed down without fail because my people have fought the good, strong, excellent fights of faith, while having been faithful in the works that I have assigned to them, declares God. It is one thing to have faith, but it is highly commendable to be faithful and diligent in the works of the Kingdom of God through steadfast commitment and devotion unto me. I, the Lord thy God, implore my people to seek not titles or prestige. Instead, they are to put forth diligent efforts to seek my presence. I raise up and exalt those that are faithful unto me whether they are abasing or abounding, abiding in plenty, or barely surviving in temporary lack. I alone am God, and my word never returns to me void. Shout Hallelujah, for I have opened the doors of unthinkable provision over your head, declares the Lord Almighty!

Dearly beloved children, be not moved by what you see, for everything that is seen is about to change, suddenly and immediately. No matter what, I am still God and forever faithful on every accord. Leave your loved ones to me, says God, and I shall perform awesome works in their spirits that shall cause their bodies, full countenance, and souls shine as celestial lights. In essence, all will know that it was I- Jehovah Shalom (The God of Peace) that touched and changed those lives, hearts, minds, bodies, and souls from the inside out. Rest and abide in me- the Lord of Hosts, while leaving all those things and people that burden you and tax your soul to me. I created them also, and I will inspire remarkable turnarounds in them, thus says the Lord God Almighty.

Allow your words to be few, yet when you speak, speak only that which I have imparted so that you will glorify Me—God Almighty, while edifying humanity. The way has been paved and the wheels set in motion for the words of your mouth to make the mountains of your soul and circumstances crumble down to rubble, declares God Almighty. Expect no less than the best, and remove the limitations off yourself, by way of stagnant thought patterns and trauma. Your faith in the Faithfulness of God opens the gateway for possibilities and opportunities without measure.

Expect the unexpected! Be still and know that I am God and far greater than all circumstances and situations. Because you have opened your hands and released your affairs of the heart to me, while casting all your cares upon mine shoulders, watch me work the miracles on your behalf flawlessly. Mine Sovereign Word never returns void. I, the Lord thy God shall bring about such intense conviction upon those that have spitefully used and misused my people, they will have no choice other than to repent and correct their wrongs as they come into proper alignment with the Spirit Divine. Give unto Me, the Lord God Almighty-- all praise and thanksgiving; for your breakthroughs and Divine Interventions have arrived. Rest and abide in me, for I am the Lord, an ever-present help at all times throughout your journey.

Amen.

Wednesday Morning
15 October 2003 @ 0620 Hours

Hallelujah! Glory and Honor unto the Lord God on High, for He is a God of more than enough! As we are called to worship the Lord thy God in spirit and in truth today and each day of life, grace abounding is with us at every turn and step of the way.

Truly I say unto thee, declares the Lord of Hosts- no stone shall be left unturned. I am the Author and Finisher of your faith indeed! Anyone that has suffered grave, unspeakable losses due to unfathomable atrocities spurning from the Divine Calling upon their lives, they shall receive great harvests for the seasons of hardship endured, proclaims God. I am a God of Recompense and I reward the diligent, faithful Sons and Daughters who worship in Spirit and Truth. When I impart a word of knowledge into my available, and attentive people, it is my desire for them to meditate on that which they heard, then they shall not be left ignorant and in the dark. The people perish where there is lack of vision, harmony within self, peace, love, and clear understanding. The mysteries to the deep shall be both unveiled and unfolded at the proper time. Continue in diligence of my works and your prayers so that you may be in correct alignment when Divine Opportunities arrive. I am God and I reward those who are faithful and pure at heart.

Come unto me, all ye' that are heavy laden, and I will give you rest and restoration. Do not get weary in well doing, for you will reap a grand harvest suddenly, providing you do not faint or give up, while continuing to walk upright in the midst of the believers and unbelievers alike, says God. Beware of those who only possess a cloak of religion, for they may fool some of the people, says God, yet I know all, see all, and hear all. Everything that is said in the confines of one's home is still not private because there is nothing that escapes the

Spirit of the Lord Almighty. They walk about using my name in vain and their ways are not blameless, their hands are not clean as they are guilty in shedding blood of their fellow brothers and sisters, because their hearts are not pure. They so callously mock and ridicule my people, slander and malign their fellow brethren, and throw rocks while hiding their hands! Yet, they are still deceived and believe that no one hears or sees them, says God. Nothing that is done in the darkness by those with hearts of darkness shall stay hidden, says God, and no stone shall be left unturned!

By the words of their mouths and faith of their spirits, trusting in Yahweh faithful and True- let thy minds be healed, delivered, and set free, declares the Lord of Hosts. I am Jehovah Rapha- the Lord God that heals. Cast all care and hurts upon me, the Lord thy God and I shall heal my people everywhere they are hurting and have been hurt. I fashioned my people in mine image- marvelous and wonderfully created in splendor. So, there is nothing impossible for me. I am the Lord God Almighty and I always reward faithfulness that is birthed out of purity of heart and reverence unto me. *(Moment of Meditation)* ... My mercy, grace, and favor shall follow you all the days of your life, says God, and you shall dwell and abide in My Presence- the Lord your God forever and ever.

Expect the unexpected and prepare for the miraculous interventions. Gifts and love offerings shall be sown into you because I have turned up my light in you. Direct communications are to be anticipated, so listen more than you speak, says God. Allow me- God of the Universe, to give you the proper words to speak so that nothing but the best fruit shall pour forth out of your spirit. Divine Connections shall seek you out. Brace yourself for overflow, for you are in right standing with me, the Lord God Almighty over all creation.

Amen

Thursday Morning
16 October 2004 @ 0655 Hours

Glory unto the Lord God on High, for awesome are His works indeed. As we, worship God is spirit and in truth, there is a mark of servitude unto the Kingdom that brands the heart of every believer who is diligent and faithful to the works of Almighty God. Trust and believe me at my word, remain steadfast in your faith-walk with me, and you shall be rewarded greatly, says God.

Be not dismayed, declares the Lord of Hosts because there is no place that you have found yourself that I did not make provisions for you to be there. Because I have ordered, guided, and directed the footsteps of those who answered My Call upon their lives, the unbreakable covenant has been established and I always provide for they that are faithful, diligent, and sensitive to the Holy Spirit. Therefore, I beseech ye' to not allow My instructions to stand ignored, while engaging in no perverse speech, for the people are held accountable for every idle word that they utter, whereas words have the power to erect and destroy. *(Moment of Meditation)* ... In all thy ways, declares God, acknowledge and revere me, for you are granted access to Wisdom Keys within My Kingdom.

Once the people begin to recognize that they are not paupers, they will be unwilling to accept less than what I have set aside for them, declares God. There is no one in My Kingdom that has truly submitted his or her lives, ways, and will unto me that I have not provided for. I am a prayer-answering, miracle-working God and I am forever faithful indeed.

Tell the truth and put the enemy to flight! For what does light and darkness have in common, inquires God? Absolutely nothing! Wherever light enters and invades, the darkness must flee because the two entities cannot cohabitate. Sow seeds of faith, faithfulness, mercy, patience, grace, and thanksgiving at all times. In your times of distress, I shall deliver you from unfathomable calamities. Those who have sown good seeds with purity of heart shall reap bountiful harvests in their own due season. Not every person has the same due season as another. *(Moment of Meditation)* ... Each person is strongly encouraged to tell the truth so that they are not falsely accused of flattery, while working out their own salvation from within, for the gods and goddesses that they were created to be from the foundations of the beginning—at the core of their existence abides their eternal Hope of Glory.

That which strengthens the person's spirit, soul, and mind also strengthens the body. However, to feed the hungry person's body when they are weak and feeble is also spiritual. For what good is it to preach at a person and not administer practical aid in areas of affliction? Those that have made a steadfast decision to follow me, the Lord of Hosts, while abandoning and losing all that they deem precious for the working out of the weighty matters in mine kingdom shall always be provided for. I grant seed to those who sow generously into the needs of others, and bread unto those who give to the downtrodden. Those who have purity of heart and willingness to do what is right simply because it is the right thing to do--- great are their rewards from God Almighty! Everything that has been stolen from the people of God, who strive to walk upright in their ways, shall be restored in abundant measure, declares God.

Be still and know God Most High is forever faithful and true. Love covers a multitude of hurt, so lift up your heart to me for repair, restoration, and replenishing. I have turned my peoples' anger into passion and their hurts into strength, for they who are determined to stay the course. Strength is required and mercies overflowing to love, forgive, and release those that have maligned you. I am the Lord God Almighty and I shall do all these things through renewed grace and love. ***Hallelujah! Amen***

Friday Morning
17 October 2003 @ 0715 Hours

Hallelujah! God has declared that this day be a day of excellence and whatever is to be done shall be done to the best of our abilities. Therefore, when having done all that you can, and putting forth your absolute best efforts, arise to profess to Me- the Lord of Hosts that you have done everything within your abilities to accomplish the tasks that have been assigned. Truly, the races are not granted to the swift or the battles to the strong, yet great measures of grace are bestowed upon those who have endured. So, let not your heart be troubled when you have done all that you can, having gone extra miles and beyond the normal call of duty for troublesome, difficult, self-absorbed people. Many do not recognize that they have a problem or are problematic to others. They are caught up in everything that suits their own purposes, while having not discerned their direct impact on others. They may be well meaning but their lack of follow-through to complete a mission unless they see tangible benefits / amenities to escalate their personal agendas. Therefore, be not weary in well doing, for there are great harvests and rewards for everything done with love and well-being of humanity in the forefront, without regard for one's own personal feelings. Do not become sidetracked by seeking directions from others who are making it up as they go along. Yet, stay focused on me- the Lord God Almighty, while abiding in peace until I work out details of all circumstances and situations. The more my people submit to me wholeheartedly in allowing the Holy Spirit to serve as their guide while pruning them of all that is unnecessary for their journey, the greater position they shall be elevated when the condition of their hearts abides in peace and harmonious relationship with God the of their soul. Whether abasing or abounding, know that I am still God, whether it be day or night.

Blessed is the name of the Lord forever more! Hallelujah! God Almighty is worthy to be praised! Behold! I have not given unto mine precious people the spirit of fear or doubt, but of power, love, and a sound mind. Be dutiful in those tasks that I have assigned, and you shall see the hands of the Lord thy God move mightily on your behalf. Watch me as I work while proving unto you once again that I am your God, Healer, Protector, Provider, Deliverer, and your rock in weary lands, shelter in the times of storm. e. Know without doubting that I am God and I have not sanctioned you to be anywhere that I had not already predestined. As you are led by the voice of Spirit Divine from within--- you have been purposed to prosper and reign, whereas the Grace of God Almighty shall filter out impurities, doubts, and negativity, that are by-products of human opinion polls. Therefore, pay particular attention to what you allow to infiltrate your livelihood, says God. The people are either feeders of the problem or contributors to the solutions. Inquire of me- the Lord of Hosts and I shall reveal to you the exact role each one plays in your life! *(Moment of Meditation)* ...

Tell the truth and shame the enemy, says God. Guard your hearts and keep your words to a minimum, saying only that which is absolutely necessary, while leaving the rest to fall away. The limelight serves as distraction, yet all things are exposed at the proper time, as each person will not be able to escape their own misdeeds and wrongdoings. When I- the Lord God Almighty holds up a mirror and shows each person pictures of himself, plays back the film in slow motion, bringing all things back to remembrance that they failed to make right, they soon begin to recognize how much more work is to be done within their beings to become effective in the ministry of reconciliation.
(Moment of Meditation) ...

Treat all people, as you would desire to be treated, for there are gracious rewards for the grace and mercy of God that is extended to others. Keep yourselves in faith and serve as walking, living epistles of God, with testimonies that shall confound the worldly wise and lead them into all truth and knowledge as to who they are. My people are to serve as pillars of light that shine throughout the darkness to draw the lost and dying, hurting and hopeless that they may come to know God for themselves. For Grace is the gift that keeps on giving. In all the peoples' searching, they are to ask for understanding and I- the Lord God shall reveal mysteries of the deep unto those who have stepped outside of the shallow waters.

Tell the truth and shame the enemy. Give your best, forget the transgressions against you, and forgive with a heart of love and thanksgiving, for God Almighty is the Lover of your soul. Give praise, honor, and glory to the Lord of Hosts- for this is a day of Divine Appointments and Supernatural Interventions, while Impeccable Communications are on the forefront. The Spirit of the Lord God Almighty abides here! *Grace and Abounding Peace...*

Amen

Saturday Morning
18 October 2003 @ 0935 Hours

Glory Hallelujah! God had proclaimed this day as a day of Diving Visitations and Supernatural manifestations! Behold! I have brought you to the place where you can bear witness to my redemption power, declares God. You have been redeemed, made to rise up, profess what I have imparted into you, speak light into the dark places, while holding the hands of they that are lost and confused, that they may bear witness to the glory and salvation of the Lord thy God, where burdens are removed, and yokes are destroyed. No matter what has been said and done, I have shielded you from the vile threats of the those in darkness. This is a day of Divine Transitions as the Holy Spirit has sanctioned and arrested the loved ones of families torn in spirit where they are drawn back into the Divine Will of God. I am the Lord of Hosts and the effectual fervent prayers of the righteousness of God avails much.

Many naysayers' tend to ramble on about the woes and circumstances of my people. However, the people that I have called and approved according to my name are to pay no particular attention to the opinions of humanity concerning the Divine Purpose for their lives. Trust only in me, declares God- for I have already paved the way for my people and the provisions have been made. The just / righteous shall live by faith in God and the grace and mercies of God are more than sufficient. I am the Lord of Hosts, I specialize in impossibilities, and there is nothing too difficult for me. My promises are always yes and amen. Favor, mercy, and grace unto the precious people of God in abundance as they are covered in unconditional Love. Those who are diligent and steadfast in the Divine Works of God for their lives shall be rewarded greatly by way of kingdom principles and precepts.

Rejoice, all ye' people that are of heavy hearts, for the Spirit of God comes forth to set the captives free. Be not dismayed by those that have broken faith, covenant, trust, and promises with you because I- the Lord God Almighty have come to set the records straight and to bring justice to those that have been egregiously wronged. *(Moment of Meditation)* ...

I am the Lord of Hosts and I decree miracles, breakthroughs, and divine appointments scheduled for my people while having commanded wealth and favor into the hands of those that have dared to take radical steps of faith while others have hung out on the sidelines and criticized the workings of God through religion, traditions of man, and legalism. *(Moment of Meditation)* ...

Those that have proven faithful are being elevated from the valleys of repose, making not waste of anything given, while in the land of the living-- and speaking life into those who feel as the walking dead. My people are to receive their daily rations of power from me- the Lord of all Glory and command that which is withered to thrive and become fruitful once more.

Embark upon the banks of the covenant seed; from the ashes emerges clarity without condemnation, bright complete recompense with family restoration. Behold! This day brings about change, outside the familiar and immersed in the peculiar and strange. I am the Lord thy God that strengthens and heals. So, receive on this day the partitions of grace because the struggles to win this race are over-- as my people have been empowered with the victory easily. I- the Lord God Almighty abides with mine people through their faith and faithfulness unto me where there is sanctity and sanity beyond their falls and failures.

To whom much is given, much more is required. As this utterance and content is Divinely Inspired, watch Me- the

Lord of Hosts works all things out and no sacrifices that have been made shall be in vain. For I reward the faithful ones in the droughts, famines, and rains. Holdfast to all that I give on this day, for I the Lord thy God have proclaimed ways out of seemingly dead ends. Handle the weak in spirit with diligence and care; love and forgive they that have wronged your hearts and I shall deliver you into the exalted places. Grace unto you, for this is birthed through much adversity and shall deliver others by way of testimony. Blessed and mighty indeed are the Sovereign Name and word of the Lord, for the ministry of reconciliation is on the rise. Let they that are redeemed through the grace and mercies of the Lord God Almighty boldly stand up and say so!

On this day, declares God, I have given unto you a stamped, signed, and sealed covenant and no stone shall be left unturned. Whatsoever thing that I have decreed, so be it established forever more, for My Word never returns void. Prepare for the outpouring of all things fruitful. As my people keep themselves available to me- the Lord of Hosts, I shall speak to and through them Divine Things. Should anyone reject my prophets- not to be mistaken for those "prophets-for- hire"—otherwise deemed as ***"Pulpit Pimps"*** -- whom prostitute doctrine, writ, and text to deceive and manipulate the people for ill-gotten gain, they shall be dealt with accordingly. The time has come to separate the flowers from the weeds and the fruits from the parasites!

Be of good courage and boldly proclaim that because I am God- I am far greater than every circumstance and situation. So, may the Glory of the Lord rise among my people, while my grace and mercy lead the way, in all matters. Rejoice always, declares God as I show up mightily in the lives of those who worship in Spirit and Truth. It is not by might, nor by power, but by and through my Holy Spirit that the captives are set free.
Amen

Saturday Night
18 October 2003 @ 2230 Hours

The Highest Praise unto Almighty God, for marvelous are the Greater Works of Divinity indeed! Whatsoever the Lord has decreed, so shall it be, for the promises of God unto those who have an ear to hear and abide in Spirit and Truth are steadfast. Those who stand firmly rooted in the faithfulness of God shall not be led astray, whereas darkness and destruction shall not prevail.

At this very hour, declares God, I am up to spectacular things, making every vision and provision readily at your disposal. Remain diligent and steadfast in those works that I have assigned unto thee for the building up of the Kingdom of God. Then I shall show you great and mighty wonders, where all will know that the Spirit of the Lord is upon you and with you, through the power of your testimony and inner workings of God Almighty in your life! I am the Lord Jehovah God and great is my faithfulness indeed. I am your rock, sword, and shield. So, when having done all that you can, stand on my word and know that my word shall never return void, proclaims God. The victory has already been won, so do not become discouraged by what is presently seen, because everything that you see now is subject to change in the blink of an eye.

I shall grant unto you in astounding measure- Wisdom that surpasses the great elders of ancient times, while imparting into the depths of your being—awe inspiring music for new songs! Though weeping may have endured for long seasons, rejoicing comes in the morning light and breaking of new days. The joy of the Lord is your strength and harvests for every hardship are received. Be not weary in well doing, declares God, for harvest time has arrived. The harvest season shall be unlike any that have ever been seen before, says God. So, borrow some vats to catch the overflow and distribute and disburse it as directed by the Holy Spirit. *(Moment of Meditation)* ...

Expect the unexpected, says God- for I will not do things the way that you anticipate, but shall do the new and unusual. As you have knocked and sought with all fervency of spirit, I have answered you!! You—dear one, are required to be the tabernacle and sanctuary to those that I send to you. Submit your will and speech unto me- the Lord your God, so that everything that is said will be in proper alignment to the assignments bestowed upon you. Commit your will unto me and I shall grant you the desires of your heart.

I- the Lord thy God am restoring unto you that which was deemed as lost. Watch -- as I perform miracles and manifestations on your behalf. May the joy of the Lord be with you every step that you take, all the days of your life!

Amen

Sunday Afternoon
19 October 2003 @ 1425 Hours

Hallelujah! God has declared this day marks the beginning of
a new season. It is turnaround time, declares the Lord of
Hosts! The victory has already been won and the war is over,
so sound the tambourine, trumpets, and let there be singing
and music all over the land! Now is the time to REJOICE,
regardless of how things may appear, proclaims the Lord of
Hosts! No matter what happened in the past, this is a new
and fruitful season, so be not dismayed if things still look the
same. Instantaneous miracles, blessings, and breakthroughs
overflowing are being released and unveiled. The seasons of
hard labor are over and the fields that have been tilled and
sweated over are about to yield incredible harvests never
imagined before, says God. You have been faithful in the
famine and continued to praise me in the wilderness, so now
the time has arrived for you to receive the good of the land.

My people that acknowledge me in all their ways, despite the
many atrocities of human sufferings, I have still heard and
heed their cries and abided in their praises, says God The
races are not won by the swift, neither do the battles go to
the strong, but unto they who have endured and fought the
good fight of faith in me, the Lord of Hosts. Get ready for
magnificent promotion, says God- for the hardships and
adversity were the testing periods that set the stage, building
integrity and faithfulness. *(Moment of Meditation)* ...

Despite all obstacles and hurdles, you have been faithful-
even during the periods where your hope went on an
extended vacation and your faith took hiatus, I- the Lord thy
God am still with you throughout the turmoil and troubles of
your soul. While chaos broke out all around you. I- the Lord
God Almighty carried you all the way. I have decreed that
you are more than an over-comer and victorious through
your God and Faithful Creator. Unto those who endured,

followed the instructions given, and delivered specified messages when their own situations seemed hopeless, surely, they have not been forgotten, yet being openly rewarded. However, I- the Lord God Almighty was processing these precious vessels for greatness because they are called to walk by faith, not by sight, and lean not to their own understanding. Although mocked and ridiculed, I have raised these set vessels up for such a time as this, as they have managed to overcome, disregarding the opinions of others about their lives, and calling of God. I am the Highest God and those that I have called, approved, and appointed, I also equip and empower with all necessary provisions to do my works in unusual ways! Yet, this is only the tip of the iceberg, declares God.

Those who worship me- the Lord thy God in Spirit and Truth shall never be brought to ruin, while every assignment of darkness is sent back upon the enemies and adversaries of those who have thrown rocks and hidden their hands, while cloaking themselves in facades of religion. Those who plot the downfall, destruction, and public humiliation of the prized Sons and Daughters of God Almighty shall be silenced by way of the sword and annihilated by the works of their own hands and the weapons that they used to crucify my people, unless they repent. The enemy is a liar, for my people are chosen for such a times as this to do what is required of them! Wherefore, nothing shall separate them from the love of God.

Be of courageous heart and steadfast faith, says God- for I am about to crumble the mountains and walls of those fortresses to rubble, right before your very eyes and you shall see the salvation and recompense of the Lord your God poured out within and through you. Render unto the Lord God Almighty all Thanksgiving, Honor, and Praise for the grace and mercy that brought forth restoration and wholeness within.

Amen

"Eyes in the Storm"

Utter **Confusion**, though it may seem,
Not withheld from the brink of these things,
Somehow not perceived as it is so,
Yet, in the midst of it all,
One should **KNOW**, that everything that can be seen,
Is yet subject immediate to change.

May sound strange,
Yet direct transcription from the Highest Authority who
reigns.
The clouds dissipate,
And hesitation takes flight,
Through another time and place,
Though still not erased from the soul,
While **GOLD** is on the border,
Of horizons unknown.
Somehow, those without a voice,
Did not rejoice when it **Rained**,
And wallowed in the temporal pains,
Of false senses of reality!

They built houses made of glass,
And dwelt with those **under-class** Spirits…
Impoverished by lack of revelation knowledge and true
unbelief.
Restoration and breakthroughs,
For the days anew,
Arriving on the shores,
Of what was no more,
Then passing tribulations,
And subject to sudden expiration…

Freedom abounds,
And without a mark, trace, or sound,
It was over,
Before it even began,
In no other place than a battle for the mind!

Written By: C. K. FORD
Monday, January 07, 2002

Monday Morning
20 October 2003 @ 0540 Hours

Hallelujah! The tidal waves of the anointing and Holy Spirit pounds the banks and vessels that have stood on the shores awaiting change, anticipating all chaos, destruction, and discord to be wiped away. On this day, declares the Lord of Hosts, I shall move by my spirit in the lives of my faithful and dutiful people. They will clearly see that I am Lord over all or God over none. *(Moment of Meditation) ...* I am the God that makes impossibilities possible. I have gone out before my people to straighten out all things that seem awry; so let not what you see dissuade you from abiding in that which I have spoken unto you. declares God. Everything that is seen is subject to change suddenly and immediately, but not hastily, for haste makes waste, says God. This is not the time to throw in the towel of defeat, for the victory has already been won. Wait for the sounding of the alarm and the announcement to be made that you are hereby declared the champion and victor of God in completeness. Because I alone am Jehovah God, I always have the last word, so on this day- decide whose report you shall believe and what master you will serve!

Let not your heart be troubled, for I- the Lord thy God have established covenant with you and my word shall not return void. Those things that I have done before, I will continue to do. The way may seem glum and bleak, but do not be deceived by smoke screens and mirrors. Many are practicing the cloak and dagger scenarios and lay in hiding, awaiting the appointed of God to pass their way so that they may attack. However, those that I have hand selected I also protect and defend. All that have dared to wage war against my people physically, emotionally, financially, or spiritually have signed their own death warrants and shall be deemed as the walking dead- unless they repent and turn from all malice, debauchery, idolatry, and wickedness of every sort.

The people that I have called according to my holy name are to be of forgiving hearts and give all their hurts to me, for I am the Lord God that heals, saves, delivers, and sets the captives free. Those appointed of God shall not be brought down low to be left in the dust, but humbled, purified through the fires of consecration and then raised up to high places through their faithfulness, integrity, excellence in character, and purity of heart. Many are the afflictions of the righteous, but the Lord thy God delivers them from it all.

Tell the truth and put the enemies to shame, forcing the assignments of darkness to flee, says God. There is freedom and liberty in the truth and knowledge of God. This is a sign of the times where people will stand up for what is wrong and evil, while rejecting that, which is righteous and pure. This shall serve as evidence of a depraved, corrupt, and deceived generation. *(Moment of Meditation)* ...

Stay on one accord with the Holy Spirit from within and allow the flow of empowerment to work through you so that you may all be in the perfect will of Jehovah God. Take care to remain sensitive to the Holy Spirit and I- the Lord of Hosts shall lead my people into revelation, sending forth the those who have sought me and have made themselves available to become vessels of honor, enabling me to speak through them to set the captives free, says God. Write the visions and make them plain, declares God. My Sovereign decrees shall not return void but shall establish all that it has been sent forth to accomplish.

Hallelujah and Amen!

Tuesday Morning
21 October 2003 @ 0605 Hours

Glory Hallelujah! Rejoice ye' people that are hard pressed, heavy burdened, beat down, financially distraught, and emotionally battered, declares the Spirit of the Lord. This is the season of total and complete restoration, and it shall be unlike any other that the people of God have ever seen before! Just because this day has started like so many before it and it is still dark outside, when the light of the morning breaks forth in the eastern sky, you shall proclaim that marvelous are the works of God Almighty indeed. You shall witness the salvation and mercy of the Lord of Hosts upon your households as Spirit paves the way for all things needed.

Those who seek My Presence, says God, even when they are worn and torn in mind, body, and spirit- I shall show myself to them on this day, as they allow Divine Guidance to lead them to wherever they are supposed to be, at the proper time. Without a test, there would be no testimony. I, the Lord of Hosts deliver my people by way of faith into overflowing grace, and from redemption to revolution. The harvests seasons have arrived, and the fruits of abundance are pouring in.

At all times, the people of God are to press into the Spirit of Truth within for Wisdom, permeated with strength, knowledge, and a spirit of excellence. Now is the time where Spirit of Divine floods those who are diligent and proven faithful with knowledge in areas where they felt weak and uncertain, or steered clear of spaces they felt inept and unworthy. However, I- the Lord God empower my people with remarkable understanding of all things that have plagued and perplexed them for years and they will not only know, but shall be able to teach, tutor, and coach others--- serving as motivators empowered of the Spirit of Truth and Revelation Knowledge! There are many unique giftings within the people of God- though some are untapped, yet now to be released for changing lives, transform thinking, and touching souls all over the world, starting with one life at a time. Through the grand outpouring and Divine Impartation of the spirit realm, there is no time like the present to believe in the remarkable faithfulness of the Lord Jehovah Divine.

My people are not to become discouraged or dismayed, for their prayers have not been ignored. The prayers of those that worship the Lord God in spirit and in truth have pierced the heart of God Almighty, causing the angels stand at attention to carry out the plans and purposes of God for their lives. The Holy Spirit has been sent forth to reach the unreachable, educate the dense and unyielding, while equipping the foolish to become wise so that they shall not continue to dash their feet against the stones by running head first into brick walls in attempt to chisel out doorways. *(Moment of Meditation)* ...

Blessed is the name of the Lord God on High, for mighty are those impeccable works indeed. Brace yourself for an overflow of revelation and waterfalls of blessing, miracles, favor, and breakthroughs. Let not your hearts be troubled and your minds are now healed by way of abiding Truth and Divine Spirit Consciousness. I, the Lord God have come to free you from the torment, pains, anxieties, and animosities. Although my precious people have been wronged, the angels have been sent to set the records straight, and no stone is left unturned. Shout Hallelujah, for the Spirit of the Lord brings clarity in the midst of confusion.

Amen.

Wednesday Morning
22 October 2003 @ 0600 Hours

Let everything that have breath praise ye' the Lord! Hallelujah! God is up to spectacular and magnificent works on this day. Therefore, we are to be in the constant flow of the spirit that we may bear a true and awesome witness to the workings of God Almighty. As surely as God has declared it, so shall it be unto us.

No matter what the dilemma or quagmire, I am God forever and there is nothing impossible or too great for me to handle; for I am the Creator and sustainer of the universe, humanity, animal, and plant kingdoms alike, while having spoken the seas and oceans into existence. I am also more than capable of establishing all that I have promised unto my people. Blessed are they whom seek the face of God and strive to live in the Divine Presence and Truth of God, for they shall have longevity of days.

On this day, when my people have given unto me- The Lord of Hosts, and fellow humanity their absolute best, I shall restore them, not only to a former state of well-being, yet to a greater degree of wholeness in me, lifting them up into awesome dimensions of flourishing grace. Those who are hungry, says God, feed their physical bodies and their spirits. The spirit that abides within is to be administered grace, mercy, and compassion, whereas the physicality of a person is to be fed tangible food that nurtures and nourishes the body. Beware of those who bear false witness against my people; many times, they are assessing a situation based on what is seen yet have not sought the presence of God for the revelation of what they should have discerned and seen through spiritual eyes. The eyes are deceived frequently by smoke screens, mirrors, cloaks, and daggers! However, the people of God must rise above their self-imposed limps and staggers, says God. Blessed is the name of the God Almighty

91

forever more. There is no need to wallow in that which has been spilled, says God. Hopefully, what has been spilled shall be a source of strength for others. *(Moment of Meditation)* ...

Rejoice, for fruitful changes are about to break forth and there shall be such a Divine Release from the spirit realm into the physical realm. Even those that deem themselves to be more accomplished and wiser, they too shall be shocked and amazed, says God. Surely, if they have a problem with the messages that I dispensed through my available, dutiful vessels of fortitude by the prompting of the Holy Spirit, then their problem is not so much with my people as it is with me- Jehovah God! Conviction is sent forth to consecrate, purify, redeem, and set things in order. Let they that have ears not only hear, responding according to their faith in me, while doing what is necessary to bring about needed changes, says God. Faith comes by hearing and hearing by the word of God.

Today, the people shall bear witness to outpouring of grace and honor, where no good thing shall be withheld from those that worship the God in spirit and in truth. Walk the path of righteousness, guarding the hearts and mouths with diligence, and I shall show up in ways that could have never been imagined, says God. Unto the obedient and pure in heart, my promises are always yes and amen. Allow your words to be few, but of pure speech for the nurturing of others so that I- the Lord Almighty may bring forth succinct message in due season! Lift up your hands and praise me continually. Tell the truth, the whole truth, and nothing but the truth- for the day is quickly approaching for my overwhelming grace to be poured out unto those that I- the Lord of Hosts have hand chosen to serve as my hands extended in the Earthly Dimensions.

Hallelujah! Amen.

Wednesday Afternoon
22 October 2003 @ 1350 Hours

Glory Hallelujah! The Spirit of the Lord has proclaimed this day as a day of Double Portions: double harvests, double empowerment, favor, miracles, manifestations, revelations, mercy, grace, wealth, and deliverance, wisdom, and truth! I am hereby pouring out my spirit upon you for the distribution and disbursement into others, says God. So, watch me and listen carefully as I confirm this truth multiple times. It makes no difference what the naysayer's say!! I always have the last word, and in the end, my people shall have the last laugh, declares God. This day, my people shall see my mighty moves of God that shall prove favorable, thus becoming recipients of wealth, wisdom, and opportunity that they never expected nor anticipated receiving. *(Moment of Meditation) ...* Because I am God, I have carved the names of my people in the Book of Life and shall connect them with willing earthly vessels in positions of honor so that the works of their hands and creative endeavors may be used in further establishing and extensions towards the building up and promotion of the Kingdom of Glory within the Earth. Anticipate the unexpected and those whose desire to remain incognito, I- the Lord of Hosts have turned up the lights in and through my precious people so that they are highly recognizable for my good works and their sincerity of heart. Blessed are the pure in heart for they shall see the presence, power, and grace of God Almighty in the land of the living.

I -the Lord of Hosts, sometimes I give my people illogical commands that defy all sound judgment. When they adhere to do those things that do not seem to make sense to the natural mind, the grip of the darkness is broken off their lives and all previously hidden things that were meant for their detriment are now exposed. Meanwhile, shackles are broken off those in right standing relationships and with the people of God. Also, scales are falling from the eyes of those who were blind. In this very hour, says God, I have set my people on course to impart words of knowledge and messages of truth to some that are in need. So, be not weary in well doing because I shall bless you in every place the soles of your feet tread.

Nondescript, half-witted notions are unacceptable in assignments for the Greater Callings of God. The people are either abiding in truth or dwelling in darkness. Those who blatantly attack my chosen Sons and Daughters without cause, other than pure spite, envy, hatred, malice, and contempt of their hearts, they set themselves up for destruction and disaster. Pride comes before the fall and those who have stood arrogantly, prideful, and haughty against my people shall reap a harvest from the seeds that they have sown. The enemy of their soul comes to deceive, steal, kill, and destroy, says God. So, why do the people of God go on self-destruction missions when they have been given the specific commands, yet chose to ignore them, inquires God?

Who can separate us from the love of God? The Love of God never fails! The time and place is hereby declared for the mighty Sons and Daughters of Valor to lift up their voices in praise so that the walls of bondage, madness, and destruction be crumbled down and laid to ruin. Let everything that have breath praise the Lord God Almighty forever more.

Hallelujah! Amen

Thursday Evening
23 October 2003 @ 1635 Hours

Glory, honor, and praise unto the Lord of Hosts! The season
of sudden change has arrived! Regardless of what present
situations dictate, the present shall take on a brilliant
dimension that will blind all those who stare directly into it.
For this dimension is certainly not for the frail or cowardly at
heart. Therefore, my people are to brace themselves and
prepare for a rushing wind similar to that of a monsoon
accompanied by heavy rains of the undeniable power flow of
spirit, bringing forth provision and protection for the
committed people of God who abide in truth and
faithfulness, proclaims God Almighty.

When my precious Sons and Daughters diligently seek me,
certainly, they shall find Me and I shall answer their cries
suddenly and immediately. Know above all else that I, the
Lord thy God am forever faithful indeed and never will I
leave or forsake my people. I am with and within you always,
even unto the ends of the creation.

Divine revelations shall pour forth, for I have imparted my
power and grace abounding into those who dare to worship
me in spirit and in truth, says God. For I am an ever-present
help at all times. Do not grow weary in well doing, yet in all
things give thanks- for gratitude increases your capacity to
receive whatever is needed. Though the forces of darkness
and adversity has attempted to wreak madness, havoc, chaos,
and destruction, it is wisdom of God's people to build their
houses on the rock that shall never crumble, which is me, the
Lord God Almighty. The believers of power through the
One True Living God shall decree blessings and affirmations
of faith over their homes and praying in grace for protection
and safety of their loved ones be clothed in peace, health,
wholeness, and prosperity. Rejoice, for the war has been won
and the spoils are being hand delivered to the homes of the

remnant of God. Open thy hands, for the provision comes swiftly and without fail, declares the Lord God Almighty.

Hallelujah and Amen!

Friday Morning
24 October 2003 @ 0635 Hours

Hallelujah! This is a day of rejoicing and triumph, declares Jehovah Shalom. So, may supernatural peace continue to abide within my precious people and their households. Wherever the Spirit of the Lord is, peace resonates, for Holy Ground has been established, says God. There shall be peace upon the households of the rich and the poor, providing they be of God, and where darkness and negative forces have attempted to wage war on the hearts, minds, bodies, temples, and homes of the people of God- the assignments of darkness have been commanded to vacate the premises because the enemy is illegally trespassing, exclaims God!

Let all of those that are in lack stand up and proclaim the word of Almighty God and they shall have whatever they say because the words of their mouths and fruit of their spirits shall produce the harvests that have been previously delayed, but certainly not denied, says God. Whatever the people stand in need of, says God- as a person thinks, those thoughts that they dwell on shall produce fruit in their lives, whether the fruit is good, bad, or ugly. *(Moment of Meditation)* ... From the heart flow the issues of life. The gates of destruction shall not prevail and let they that be of power, love, and sound mind vested by the Holy Spirit stand up and boldly profess the salvation, redemption, and restoration powers of Almighty God! Surely, I say unto thee, declares the Lord of Hosts, let your path and ways be observed as upright, also the meditations and motives of your hearts be pure and just. At all times, allow the words of thy mouth and meditation of thine hearts be pleasing and acceptable, producing fruit that is good for the soul

Since the beginning of time, says God, there has always been seed time and harvest time. They that have sown seeds of discord, malice, bitterness, slander, and bore false witness against their fellow brothers and sisters, says God, shall be made to eat the bread from the crops they planted. Be of good courage and a sound mind, for jealousy, envy, strife, and idle words shall be the bitter waters that shall choke the wicked, says God. They may possess a form of Godliness where they are able to fool the people, yet the spirit of truth sets all records straight and sheds light on that which is hidden.

Blessed is the name of the Highest God forever more. Be still and know that I am God and all that I have promised, I shall deliver because I am forever faithful indeed. Whatsoever thing that I have decreed, so shall it be unto my people. Pay minimal attention to those things and people that come to distract you, while filtering out all that is not edifying to the spirit. I- the Lord of Hosts have sent my word forth today to set the captives free. Therefore, be of a courageous heart and keep yourselves blameless before me because I reward the faithful, diligent, obedient, and humble, say God. Keep your words to a bare minimum today and I shall show up in unexpected ways to bring about peace that surpasses all understanding, along with provisions that shall take care of all the necessities of your livelihood, says God. I provide each vessel his / her daily rations of wisdom, increasing his love for humanity and securing the families and households of the Sons and Daughters of the God. Shout Hallelujah, for the Spirit of the Lord has spoken and brought forth manifestation, mercy, and all that is necessary.

Amen.

Saturday Morning
25 October 2003 @ 0720 Hours

Behold, declares God…for as this day has come to a bold beginning and the way has been made so that the word shall pour forth, bearing fruitful manifestations, there shall be no stone left unturned. Only the obedient, faithful, and diligent are worthy and deserving of my highest favor, honor, and blessings, says God. My grace and mercies are more than sufficient as I handsomely reward those that work for me to establish the Kingdom of God upon the Earth, proclaims the Lord of Hosts. Therefore, be of good courage and a sound mind, laying aside all that burdens you because I- the Lord thy God have decreed the beginning from the end and the end from the beginning. Those that I have established covenant with--- it is not only my obligation, but also my sincere pleasure to provide for the households of those that I foreknew. For I am their Father, Creator, and Lover of their souls. I decree unto you this faithful day, my people shall not be left without any good thing (those that worship me in Spirit of and in Truth), while all needs (physical, emotional, spiritual, and financial) shall be taken care of exactly as stated. Open your hands, witness with your mouths, and believe with your entire heart that I, the Lord God Almighty shall do all that I have decreed, and it will not come a single moment too late. I alone am an on-time God and I always come through in my own ways. I am not a man that I should lie, neither the Son of Man that I should repent. So, stand in awe and amazement as I perform an immediate work. Regardless of what it looks like or how it feels, says God, know that the ways have already been made. Let not your heart be troubled, for I shall provide unto you rest and peace in great measure.

Tell the truth and shame the enemy so that grace, peace, and wholeness shall rest and abide with and within thee, says God. Though you have been broken several times over, you have been made strong by the Holy Spirit within so that you may endure all trials and arise from the pits and snares, says God. Many are the afflictions of the righteous, but the Lord delivers them from it all. Truly, I say unto thee, it is harvest time and you shall not be made to eat the bread of shame or humiliation, but the angels shall bring shame and confusion upon the households of they that have sought to do you harms and malign you in order to build themselves up, says God. Beware of those rock throwers that claim to come bearing the choicest fruit, because they have entangled themselves in confusion, illusion, deceit, manipulation, and self-preservation, while stepping on the backs of others, says God. In essence, they are truly self-absorbed and self-serving, only coming to promote their own agendas. Be mindful of this and you will not be caught off guard, says God.

There is no hiding place; the clarion call has resounded for repentance so that the houses may be established in divine order and discipline. No stone shall be left unturned, so hold fast and witness the miracles and manifestation of Almighty God, for the due season is now. Open your mind and heart for long overdue communications; for they that have been out of touch with you for quite some time shall come to you needing some clarity and peace of mind as to how you feel, what your position is, and where they now stand, says God. Expect more than one Divine Impartation and you shall receive confirmations and blessings overflowing as the Spirit clothes you in grace, mercy, favor, and honor. Listen carefully and watch me work everything out for you today. Friends from past days will resurface. Communicate in truth and grace. The blessing of the Lord makes you wise, whole, and wealthy, while adding no strife or sorrow. Give me all the glory, for I am the Lord of Hosts and worthy to be praised.

Hallelujah! Amen

Sunday Night
26 October 2003 @ 1915 Hours

Glory unto the Lord God on High, for marvelous are His
works indeed. At this very hour, says God, I need you to
understand and believe that I- Jehovah God am bigger than
your problems, circumstances, and situations. When my
people praise and worship me in spirit and in truth, they open
the gates and windows of provision—thus causing the grace
of God to pour out everything that they stand in need of
from the spiritual realm into the physical realm, says God. I
am far greater than anything or anyone that my people have
ever seen. Unto they who are dutiful to Divine Instruction
and active in doing those things that are purposed for them
to do according to their specific calling, nothing is withheld.
No matter what my people are encountering, says God, the
power of life and death are in the tongue. Doubt not what I,
the Lord thy God have declared because I am able to open
up doors and make ways where and when my people do not
see the way, says God. The path has already been laced in
gold and I have gone before you to rectify all wrongs that
have been done unto you, says God. The way has been
cleared and you shall see the mercy and grace of the Lord
surround you and surprise you, says God. Let the joy and
salvation of the Lord be your strength and your guide.

Those that have dared to press their way into my presence at
this hour and lifted up their needs to me at the place that I
have appointed, I am well pleased and shall meet all needs,
says God. Rest in me and know that whatsoever is needed, I-
the Lord thy God have already made the way possible. Give
thanks, honor, and praise unto me, says God, and you shall
not be denied any necessary thing, for my people serve a
prayer-answering, miracle-working God. Through your faith
and faithfulness, the way has been made before and all needs
met, I shall continue to do so right now. Keep your faith up

and trust me as I deliver exactly what is needed at just the right time, says God. No weapon formed shall prosper against those that worship me- the Lord of Hosts in spirit and in truth, while acknowledging me in all of their ways.

Those that have surrendered their all unto me, I shall reward them greatly as they forgive those that have offended them, because letting go of the offenses will bring forth the blessings and provision more quickly, declares God. I am the Lord thy God, and I shall shut the mouths of the gossipmongers! They will be made to eat the fruits of shame for their words of bitterness and antagonism against the prized Sons and Daughters who strive to live peaceable lives.

My people are to prepare themselves for the overflow or grace as they have proven faithful in the small things that I have given and assigned to them, declares God Almighty. Stand up, shake off every attack, lie of the enemy, and know that the gates of chaos and assignments of darkness shall not prevail, says God. Grace abounding, and peace be unto you! For this is the day that the Lord has empowered you to thrive in, so rejoice in all gladness and gratitude!

Hallelujah! Amen

Monday Morning
27 October 2003 @ 1115 Hours

Praise the Lord! Hallelujah! God- the Lord of Hosts declares on this day, whatever my people have asked of me according to my Divine Will, it shall be given, providing they believe me at my word and by faith that I am able to do exceedingly more than they may ask or think. Those that come before me first and seek my presence and direction, I shall then step out in front of them making all the crooked places straight and rough ways smooth. The effectual, fervent prayers of the righteous Sons and Daughters avails much, say God. No matter how the enemy has tried to torment my people and keep them bound by wrong thinking, I- the Lord of Hosts have given them power to renew their minds. Those who believe by faith and are willing to do all that I instruct shall be rewarded with the good of the land, even when no good thing seems to exist in the land where they abide.

The faith and faithfulness of my people in me and unto me, declares God, has opened doors for them and all they must do is simply walk through the doors that I have opened and call upon me while believing that they have already received the provision because I have made the way possible. Keep your eyes and hearts fixed on me, the Great Jehovah God and then rejoice as the manifestations fall into place. Meanwhile, the mailbox shall also hold provisions because I promised that I would turn the negatives into positives, while overturning those things suddenly and immediately that were originally designed to bring disaster. I -the Lord thy God have caused everything to work in the favor of my people, despite previous information that was piled up against them. *(Moment of Meditation)* ... I am Jehovah God, Forever Faithful and True!

Give unto me- the Lord of Hosts, all glory, honor, and praise for I am the God of Divine Recompense. Everything that my faithful Sons and Daughters have received, says God- I have made the way possible because I am both the Creator and Sustainer of all life form and can move the hard-hearted and stingy, making them give unto my people leaving them baffled as to how or why. Trust me, know that I am God, and have clothed you in mercy, grace, and the highest favor to receive the blessing, promises, provisions, and manifestations, says God. Choose you this day what master you shall serve and whose report you shall believe.

Expect the unexpected, yet the unexpected right now is a good thing, says God. Be duly advised that you shall not be moved until I shift and move you to where I have you to go. Meanwhile, I have sent out grace and mercy ahead of you to make all rough places smooth. I am your health, help, strength, provider, redeemer, and deliverer, says God. Know that all things are possible unto they that believe in me, for I am the Lord God Almighty and worthy to be praised.

Hesitate not to extend your hands and warm heart to they that are in dire straits, says God. Rejoice while revering the redemption of the Lord you God in the land of the living! Therefore, praise me all the more, as I am forever faithful indeed.

Amen

Wednesday Morning
29 October 2003 @ 0525 Hours

Hallelujah! The highest praises unto the Lord of Hosts- for mercy and grace endures forever! Behold, for there is no time such as this present season that I- Jehovah – your Strong Tower and Fortress-- will ignite the spirit mightily from within precious people who are presenting themselves willing, available, and committed to carry forth missions for the Kingdom of God, as total dominion is established within the Earth. The time has arrived for NEW THINGS to be unveiled, that are not designed to shock and awe the people, yet to facilitate perfected divine order in the lands, homes, sanctuaries, and lives of those who worship God in Spirit and in Truth! Though many are called, few are chosen, and of they that are chosen, even fewer are willing to be sent, unless they have the approval of others and the circumstances are satisfactory and to their liking, says God. What they fail to realize, is that Divine Appointments are never designed for their convenience, personal timing, or preset agendas.

Whatever they have been required to leave behind and have lost, they shall be greatly rewarded that much more as they follow the leading of the Holy Spirit from within. Therefore, they that strive to do an excellent work, while allowing divine precedence to perfect their character and sharpen their integrity shall be brought forth from the refiners' fire as pure gold, says God. Though their friends abandon them, and their families may forsake them, never shall they be forsaken or forgotten by Lord Most High, for I am forever faithful! Truly, I say unto you, never shall my precious people be forsaken nor forgotten in their faithfulness unto The Lord of Salvation—for Love covers a multitude of hurts. The blessing of the Lord brings joy, empowers the people to abide in freedom, wisdom, and wholeness, declares God.

This day, declares God, marks a period of sudden, immediate change! Those who have wronged my people, spitefully abused, used, and misused them shall eat the fruits of their misdeeds, then shall be made to pay recompense unto those they have transgressed. The way of the transgressor is most difficult, especially when they wage war against people who have abided in peace and strived to do what is right by others. *(Moment of Meditation) ...* The people are convicted through the works of their own hands and bring condemnation upon themselves as they reap harvests from the seeds that they have sown, says God. Those who live by according to their faith in God Almighty and they faithfulness and diligence to do what is right-- the gates of darkness shall never prevail as they worship the God of their Creation in spirit and in truth. For the people may plan and work in earnest, yet Jehovah God brings forth promotion and increase.

Hallelujah! It is moving and shifting time, as every provision needed comes to fruition, and the process is without toil, heavy labor, or stress. As my people have continued to press towards the mark of their higher calling, despite their circumstances and situations, they are being elevated to places of prominent magnitude. For everything that was lost, I-- the Lord thy God, shall replace and replenish with finer and grander amenities, whereas my precious ones shall not be made to feast on the bread of shame or humiliation. Those that have travailed the roads of hardship, while having taken whatever survival measures necessary, through diligence and faithfulness in the small things, overflowing waves of increase come about through unexpected channels. May the mercy and grace of Almighty forever endure.

No more empty hands, for the faithful, humble people are now in receipt of more than enough to serve as a blessing to others, declares the Lord of Hosts. Therefore, be not weary in well doing, because the seasons of harvests begin now!

Do not succumb to dismay, for the focused and fruitful words of the lips shall produce abundance, as all things work together, establishing that which is intended and purposed of this day. Continue to Proclaim the grace and peace of the Lord, as restoration and revelation- not only in your life springs forth, also in the lives of others to come about full circle! *Amen*

Thursday Morning
30 October 2003 @ 0930 Hours

Glory Hallelujah! On this day, declares God, my people that are called by name are required to rise up while standing their ground against the world of darkness that attempts to distract and dissuade them. They shall walk in the light as they are abiding in Light! In all things, tell the TRUTH without bias and trust that truth paired with wisdom shall open doors that were previously closed! As the people of God are covered through Divine Protection, while gracing others in love, humility, truth and generosity, seeds of graciousness are sown to bring about revolution, evolution, and steadfast change. When the truth is administered in love and by grace, it shines light into the dark places and carries the power to set the captives free. In all things, be of good courage, a pure heart, and clean hands. That which does not edify- tears down and destroys. Yet, there are indeed times when many things must be torn down and destroyed, for the word of Almighty Divine is a two -edged sword- cutting of those things that must be pruned, while bringing forth life and healing after the infected tissues are removed. The healing process may not be comfortable yet proves expedient in promoting overall health to the body. *(Moment of Meditation)* ... On this day, declares God, my precious people may be required to sit on their hands to prevent the spilling of a fool's blood. Leave they that are foolish to their own devices, says God, for a fool in his / her folly shall self-destruct. *(Moment of Meditation)* ...

Shout Hallelujah! declares God, for you have been brought to a pivotal turning point in the spirit realm, so allow not your focus to be broken or distractions to overtake you. Distractions lead to destruction. So, be on guard for those that seek to antagonize and dissuade you from my mission for your life. Because I am God, I am a keeper of my word and nothing that I have decreed unto you shall return void. Do not lose the faith in The God of your very Existence, nor forfeit hope in the promises for your life, for that which has been declared is also decreed, thus being established.

Although periods of solitude have been required of you, I have brought you to this place of isolation so that perfected works in process yields great progress-- through increasing your knowledge and understanding of my calling upon your life, says God. My assignment on your life is not for the faint at heart! You were born a warrior, fighting to stay alive against all odds from the very beginning! Yet you have been cultivated in strategic warfare-- coupled with bondage-breaking, yoke-destroying empowerment to help deliver those who are bound in consciousness, as the captives are set free through the renewing of their minds. Truly, I say unto you, at all times, be diligent to that which I have assigned you to do, and you shall not fail at anything that you have been purposed to do by way of Spirit Divine within you, says God. The angels are positioned all around you so that death, harm, or destruction shall not befall you. Though many pray for your demise, I- the Lord your God have my hands upon your life, and you shall not be caught in the snares of the enemy, regardless of the traps that they attempt to set. The grace of the God brings peace, wholeness, joy and adds no sorrow.

The time has arrived, for my people to lift up their voices and clap their hands, decreeing by faith that all things are possible to they that believe and trust in the Lord God Almighty, while being steadfast and diligent in that which they have been purposed to do. Be bold and courageous, meditate upon the word that have been imparted into you, speak those messages until they become alive in your soul, and suddenly, without warning, harvest and abundance shall see you out, overflowing in astounding capacity! The Great Divine Spirit from within shall rectify all wrongs suffered, wherefore shame and disillusionment shall not be the bread that you feast upon.

Do not feel guilty nor condemned for not being in a place that people are demanding for you to show up --yet commit to being led by Spirit in all things, while doing everything necessary to show up only in the places where you have been directed you to be, says God. I am the Lord of Hosts, and I shall lead you wherever you are to be, for I hold all priority. As your footsteps are ordered, guided, and directed, prompting you in your every movement and momentum, keep in mind that if it were meant for you to be elsewhere, then that is where you would be! Reject those that seek to control, dominate, and override my purposes and mission for your life, while not being held captive by guilt and condemnation in doing so. *(Moment of Meditation)* ...

I, the Lord thy God have stretched you beyond self and outside vain imaginations of humanity so that I may extend and increase your territory to encompass those things, people, and places that were once deemed untouchable and unreachable. Take nothing that has been spoken unto you lightly, says God, for I am escorting my people who worship me in spirit and in truth into increased dimensional elevations by way of Spirit's leading. So, regardless of what anyone else has to say, I, the Lord your God have called, sent, and justified you. I dare not call those that are qualified in their own minds, yet I do qualify and empower those that I call, says God. Therefore, you have been molded and fashioned for this very hour to shine light into the darkness, confound the worldly wise, and while enlightening the foolish to bring about understanding.

As sure as you have waited, you shall now bear witness to the goodness and salvation of the Lord your God in the land of the living. Man shall not live by bread alone, but by every word that proceeds out of the mouth of God Almighty. No longer will the rock throwers be allowed to pose as obstacles lying in wait to ensnare the children of purpose, while disrupting missions for the appointed vessels of Almighty Lord. Those that have lived by the sword shall also die by the sword and shall harvest what they have planted in the lives of others. Be of good cheer, strong courage, sound mind, peaceful spirit, clarity of the soul as all things ultimately works out in your favor. They that have wronged you shall continue on the path of folly, self-hatred, and utter rebellion while having sentenced themselves to destruction crucially personified.

This is a day of Divine Visitations and do not allow yourself to get grabbed by anger, yet pray without ceasing, for the grace of God is with you always. Keep your conversation to bare minimum today, your heart blameless, your spirit gracious, and your hands free of idle works to be in position of prayer for those who are hurting. I am the Lord God Almighty and I am worthy of all praise, honor, and thanksgiving. Rejoice, for today is a day of new beginnings!

Hallelujah! Amen

Friday Morning
31 October 2003 @ 0620 Hours

Glory, Glory! The grace and magnificent presence of the
Lord thy God abides here and fills this room! Regardless of
what happened yesterday, last month, last year, or last decade,
says God, I am still with you now and forever more! My
Spirit abides with you, communing in fellowship as you are
sanctioned to reside in the fullness of Spirit presence,
regardless of the pressures of the world. I am now rewarding
and flourishing you beyond measure, declares God.
Therefore, brace yourself for the overflow is being poured
into you for the harvests that are to come! The races are not
won by the swift, or the battles given to the strong, but
victory is granted without fail to they who have endured.
Delight yourself in God always as I have in you, that shall
cause you to abound in wisdom, grace, truth, well springs of
knowledge, in addition to fruits of compassion and
generosity. Whereas, you have been tried, tested, and proven
faithful, declares the Lord of Hosts.

I- God Almighty have brought you to this place and through
these tribulations that you may embrace me to be your shelter
in the times of storm. Everything provided to you has been
bestowed by way of grace. So, be of good courage, peaceful
heart, sound mind, and fruitful spirit. Fret not over anything,
and do not waste energy on tiresome things or worrisome
people, for I have greater plans for you, and it does not
include exhausting yourself on futile missions.
(Moment of Meditation) ... As you have sought me out in the
times of feasting and famine, I have always been with you.
Therefore, you have not been abandoned or forsaken. I have
imparted into you gifting and seeds that shall bless all
humanity while glorifying the God of Creation. No matter
what has been said about you or done to you, I am still God
of your life and existence. You are upheld in the palm of my

hand, so none can harm you unless they come through me first! When they set themselves up to attack you in mind, body, spirit, emotions, and finances, they have attacked me-- the Lord of Hosts-- for I am your very present help, defender, and protector at all times!

Do not be alarmed by the pains of your heart, for I am expanding your heart to impart greater love within you, to open gates of forgiveness of the highest caliber, nurturing from the spirit, healing hands, and renewal of the body, mind, and spirit, declares God. Oftentimes, my children's pains are intensified as their capacity to receive deeper extensions of grace and thanksgiving, says God. *(Moment of Meditation)* ... I am Jehovah God and make use of those who are available to Spirit, while having been required to abandon their own agendas and itineraries, proclaim the Lord God Almighty.

Prepare for Divine Visitations, miraculous interventions, impartations of revelation knowledge, and clarity in affairs of the heart. Keep your eyes, heart, and mind focused, while bearing witness to the remarkable shifting of all that has been out of order and alignment, being brought into its precise condition and rightful positions.

Hallelujah! Amen

Friday Afternoon
31 October 2003 @ 1415 Hours

Hallelujah! All glory unto the Lord God Almighty in the here and now, as outpourings of wondrous Mercy, Grace, and Forgiveness are at an all-time high. Faithful is God Almighty, the establishment of beginning and end. Shalom, exclaims God! Peace unto you! My peace that surpasses all understanding encompasses wholeness, soundness of mind, health, posterity, and prosperity—where nothing is withheld, says God. I am the God of abundance! The curse of poverty has been broken off my people, providing they accept all that I desire for them to receive. There shall always be poor people that dwell upon the earth; however, that was not my original intent for humanity. Those that are blessed beyond measure, while abiding in overflowing capacity, are to share with those who have very little, if any. My people are to serve as the hands of compassion extended, while having a heart to share what they have for the betterment of those in seasons of crisis and dire need. They are not to hoard what they have for themselves and turning the blind eye to the destitute and downtrodden. Although they may not be able to help everyone, they are to be consistent in helping others, and this begins with those who they readily encounter in their own surroundings. How can my people expect to touch the world if they are unwilling to reach out to just one, inquires God? When my precious people reach out to feed one, clothe another, and yet encourage someone downhearted, then these things they have also done as unto The Lord Almighty. *(Moment of Meditation)* ...

Seeds of forgiveness and peace have been imparted into my people. However, the seeds are unable to grow unless they are sown and planted into others. They are not to look back on those things and people that have inflicted hurt, yet keeping their eyes focused on the Higher Calling, becoming empowered to bring healing to the land, declares God. I am

114

the Lord God Almighty and I am more than able to heal my people everywhere they are hurting, as they are required to administer healing and forgiveness into others. *(Moment of Meditation)* ...

On this day, the alarm sounds for seasons of Restoration! Rest and abide in the spirit of Truth and Love, trusting that no stone is left unturned, and the glory of God is your portion that shall not run dry. As my precious people open their hearts, the healing process occurs from the inside out, for Spirit makes way for the broken-hearted, restoring grace and benevolence to the utmost. Take caution not to allow others to dissuade or malign you, says God. At all times, my people are to tell the absolute truth without fear of repercussion. For those whom the Spirit of the Lord sets free are free indeed and the gates of destruction shall not prevail, declares the Lord of Hosts.

Territories have been established and boundaries have been drawn in the sand, but there is no hiding place for they that have thrown rocks and hidden their hands, says God. Many are the afflictions of the righteousness of God, yet the Lord of Hosts brings about liberty and peace within the soul.

As mysteries unravel and time is replenished, I shall seek out the depths of the souls seeking me- the Lord God Almighty, so that I may pour out tremendous revelations to they that are desiring to go deeper, while bypassing the typical surfaces of religious realms, proclaims the Lord Jehovah God. The Grace and Mercy of the Lord is your strength and shield, as you abide in the presence of the Lord your God forever more!

Amen

Sunday Morning {dark hours}
02 November 2003 @ 0025 Hours

All praise, thanksgiving, and honor unto the Lord Almighty, for awesome are these amazing works indeed! No matter how the circumstance or situation appears, trust that all seasons have an expiration date. The Lord your God is your strong tower and fortress indeed, forever faithful and without fail on every accord, say God. *Hallelujah!*

Glory to the Lord Almighty! The Spirit within arises making way for all that is needed. By God's mercy and grace that endures forever, we are granted the keys to the kingdom and dominion over all things that God has created. However, we are required to exercise our authority through Divine Wisdom and Insight, which empowers us in times of struggle, triumph, feast, and famine. *(Moment of Meditation)* ...

Behold! declares God Almighty. As my people walk by faith and have been enriched in their spiritual growth, I shall lead them and guide them in their journeys. Those that have learned to survive off pure, unadulterated faith and only the bare essentials have passed the tests and proven faithful on all accords. The wilderness experiences are used for the perfecting and building of character, edification, purification, and consecration, expanding the peoples' capacity to both give and receive in greater measure, says God. Those who have proven faithful are rewarded handsomely in their due season, without added toil or strife. They are to invite their closest loved ones who have stood with them through the times of hardship, to partake in the harvests. For there shall be more than enough, and their well springs shall not run dry. Nothing is impossible unto those who abide in spirit and truth, diligent in all that they have been assigned and purposed to do, according to their measure of faith and commitment, while withstanding unthinkable challenges, obstacles, and adversity that would have buried others alive, declares Jehovah God.

New and fresh territories have been expanded, excavated, and delivered unto you without strings attached, says God. So, in all things, Peace Be Still! When precious seeds from the pure at heart are sown for the betterment of others, the people then reap bountiful harvests. Open your hearts for an infusion of greater love and appreciation for the awesome workings of Spirit, as well as continual works in process. Without the processes, no progress is made. Dare not hesitate, for divine timing is crucial, as opportunities are presented to bless and minister to others, exclaims God! I - God Almighty, am not concerned about the conveniences or comforts of my people, but the condition of their souls and their handling of others. *(Moment of Meditation)* ...

Pray without ceasing, being diligent in the labors of your heart, hands, and spirit, then stand in supernatural expectancy of glorious holiday seasons that brings forth restoration on all accords, says God. The lost will be drawn out of dark places, the hurting and broken are being healed and made whole, the bound set free, as the grace of the Lord abides bountifully with you, proclaims the Lord God Almighty.

Trifold, multi-dimensional harvests shall seek my people out. Their mailboxes and bank accounts will begin to overflow with wealth, resources, and long overdue recompense as they choose to walk in the higher ways of integrity, honoring the Lord their God above all things, demonstrating love, compassion, and genuine concern for the betterment of others, purposely serving as mine hands extended, declares God. Shout Hallelujah, for the blessing of the Lord brings about the spirit of wisdom, health, wealth, and overflowing joy with adding sorrow.

Amen

Sunday Morning {daylight!}
02 November 2003 @ 0720 Hours

Grace! Grace! God's grace and mercy are more than sufficient. As we are called to worship the Lord thy God in spirit and in truth, God rewards those that diligently and faithfully serve humanity in practical helps, not just religious rituals.

As fruit springs forth bountifully from trees and branches that have been painstakingly pruned, says God- cultivation of the Holy Spirit impartation is paramount and shall produce overflow of wealth, substance, and humility. Pestilence of discord, confusion, self-hatred, greed, and idolatry breeds corruption. The people of integrity are to practice self-control so that they are not found guilty of browbeating the fellow sisters and brothers with written text and stale doctrine, while not leading by example and failing to abide in peace, grace, and generosity. Faith comes by hearing and hearing by the Word of God- not with physical ears, but spiritual discernment and humility, being readily available to be of service in the places they are able to make a difference. Even the brothers and sisters that have not yet accepted the invitation of salvation shall reap the benefits of the blessing and principles of God. *(Moment of Meditation)* ...

Seed time and harvest time is not just applicable to the Kingdom of God, but are universal laws established by the Creation. God said- "Let there be light!" The light manifested through the spirit and words spoken of God bringing forth Universal Light that shines until this day. Therefore, whatever a person says of themselves and perceives of self, these words shall also produce the fruit thereof. My people are to take extreme care in allowing the words of their mouth and meditation of their hearts to be pleasing and acceptable as to not spurn creations that are ill-intentioned.

The races are not won by the swift, or the battles given to the strong, but to they who endure to the end while fighting the good fight of faith. Endurance produces strength and reveals character, says God. My people are to be molded and pressed by the workings of the Holy Spirit from within so that humility and grace creates perfected works that bypass the worldly forms of excellence, declares the Lord of Hosts. *(Moment of Meditation)* ...

Be encouraged and hold fast; for they that have counted my people out, kicked and underestimated them, disparaged the power of Spirit in their lives, shall be made to bear witness to all that is being done for the families that worship God in Spirit and in Truth, says God. The joy of the Lord shall serve as my people's strength, as their victory is secured through their faith and faithfulness unto me- the Lord God Almighty. Those that worship God in spirit and truth shall be completely restored before they are able to contemplate all the details! For I alone am God and great is my faithfulness indeed!

Amen

Monday Morning
03 November 2003 @ 0610 Hours

Praise, thanksgiving, and honor unto the Lord thy God. This day marks a time of sudden change, declares God, and nothing shall remain as it was before or as it is now. Divine Turnaround Seasons bring forth an immediate twist, says God. Therefore, expect the unexpected, but anticipate nothing in the familiar, whereas, embarking upon the delightfully peculiar is paramount, says God. Let not your hearts be troubled by what you see now, as everything that you are currently seeing shall dissipate into places far away and times long ago. Crossover into the supernatural shall come quickly, while catapulting people of truth into greater dimensions than they have ever known. The preparation for excellence in all things has proven fruitful, yet painful. Let not what appears to be hopeless steal your joy and cause you to doubt, for those that have been delivered into peace and clarity of mind, being declared them as triumphant on every accord, shall reap the good of the land, proclaims the Lord of Hosts.

Lift up Holy Hands, those of you who worship me in spirit and truth and praise me anyhow, says God. Hallelujah Anyhow- for the gates of darkness shall not prevail. The building of sustained patience is a painful process for the vessels of God. Although they have been shown the ending, it is their deepest desire to sprint towards the finished line to collect the prize. However, they are being processed thoroughly for greater empowerment, imbued with wisdom and temperance, carefully handling the gifts cultivated within for the service of humanity. Therefore, do not grow weary in well doing, for you shall come out on the other side, proving stronger and more agile than before the times of testing began. The gifts are discovered, revealed, and received through the perfecting of grace and thorough cleansing of all debris and clutter. For they shall not receive anything filthy and vile in spirit while being bound in deception and confusion.

Today is a day of Divine Interventions! Therefore, in all that is done, the people are to keep themselves blameless, and their speech pure, and their words to a minimum. I will show up in ways unexpected—while bringing those troublesome situations to a screeching halt. Now, graciously receive the remarkable manifestations of significant change. Communications are overflowing as waters in a flood zone, as those that reach out will speak in clarity and truth. Nurture the broken, for when my people nurture the broken ones back to health and sanity, so shall their family members and loved ones be healed in the process.

Give glory, honor, and praise unto me- Jehovah God, for the Spirit of the Lord has come to set the records straight.

Amen

Wednesday Morning {*dark*}
05 November 2003 @ 0445 Hours

Praise the Lord! Hallelujah! Amen! Grace, Grace! Glory abounds as the Spirit of the Lord comes to set the captives free and push back every assignment of darkness ever known to the families of God and Kingdom Relations, declares the Lord of Hosts. No stone shall be left unturned, as the darkness flees quickly. My people are not to look upon their lives through clouded vision or hindrances in the forefront but are to trust in God Eternal. The darkest hours are just before dawn, so the precious people are to guard their minds and hearts with all diligence, abiding in the truth and substance of spirit, that their hope is not lost.

Let all whom believe by way of Spirit upon the Lord Jehovah God, raise their hands in total reverence right now, while focusing on the goodness of God in the land of the living. The time has now arrived, to take a stand and shine light into the darkness. The visions have not been aborted, and everything is being turned around quickly in excellence. Therefore, choose ye' this day whose report you shall believe and what master you shall serve. I have not brought you thus far to leave you. It matters not if the parasites have come to devour the fruit from your orchards because the pesticide of the Spirit from within shall charge forth to eradicate all pests, rodents, and assignments of darkness that have attempted to rob you of your harvests. Right now, all things are being shifted into proper order, says God.

They that have taken extended leaves of absence from the truth of their calling are being pulled into rightful positions through renewing of their minds. No longer will they be allowed to wallow in less than the Divine Creations of Spirit, Light, and Truth, being called to come up higher and go deeper into Spirit to in the fullness of their Divinity from the inside out. *(Moment of Meditation)* ...

I am the Lord God Almighty and I give unto you peace and joy unspeakable, along with cleansing and wholeness. There is healing in my presence of Spirit and grace in overflow is more than sufficient. I am the Lord of Hosts-- Lover of the broken, battered, and worn. Even when they are cracked and marred, I mold, reshape, sculpt them into fortified works of art to be used towards the betterment of Creation. The Spirit of Jehovah God restores and renews lives, re-establishing foundations from the cornerstone and internal frameworks of architecture. Shout Hallelujah, for the joy of the Lord is your strength indeed!

Amen

Thursday Afternoon
06 November 2003 @ 1255 Hours

Praise and Thanksgiving abounds on this day! The Spirit of the Lord abides here, and every assignment of darkness is rendered null and void, declares God Almighty! The clocks have been stopped, time itself has been pushed back, and those things have been done to the people of God by those who have an axe to grind- are being undone via the Spirit of Truth and Peace. The evildoers that have patted themselves on the back and praised themselves for all the havoc and chaos wreaked in the lives of others—their efforts shall be disintegrated quickly, declares God.

In all the peoples' ways, acknowledge the Great I AM in spirit and truth, trusting that all things are working together for the greater good in their lives. There are times when it is required to leave behind all that is familiar to, pulling up the hems of your garments and tread to higher ground. If those that proclaim a desire to help are not serving as investors into my visions to empower and uplift others, then they pose as hindrances and obstacles. *(Moment of Meditation)* ...

When the moon overshadows the sun and, a solar eclipse occurs, and the world grows dark for a season. The darkness must flee by the power of the Holy Spirit within my people as they operate in the authority of the divinity within them. These are principle truths that set the captives free, for only those things established and fortified in truth and wisdom shall remain, withstanding the tests of time! Although the Kingdom of God suffers violence, the violent and those violated shall take it all back by force proving victorious in the endeavors of faith, through sound wisdom and divine guidance.

Time out for toiling and weeping over treacherous situations, for the demolition of every obstacle and roadblock that has attempted to impede the visions of those of purposeful intention and integrity-- begins NOW. Those who have dug pits for others out of spite, jealousy, greed, and malice, are being buried alive in unmarked graves. Therefore, my people should not find it shocking when they hear of funeral processions, as those who are spirit dead are deemed as walking dead, proclaims the Lord of Hosts.

Will the _**true scribes**_ of the God Almighty boldly stand up to go forth and deliver the divine messages to an obstinate, rebellious people? The true scribes are they who are set apart, fashioned to be quick listeners, yet slow to speak unto they have received clarity in truth and knowledge that bypasses the obvious, declares God Almighty. Therefore, they continue to carry on despite their adversities, while fanning the torch to illuminate the dark places of the world with ministry letters given unto them for the betterment and illumination of humanity, says Jehovah God. The visions are yet for the appointed time and that appointed time is now. Shout Hallelujah, for I- Jehovah God Divine have spoken on this day.

**Hallelujah! Amen**

Friday Morning
07 November 2003 @ 0710 Hours

Hallelujah! On the seventh day, signs and wonders come about. Therefore, be not amazed at the works of God Most High- remarkable revelations and manifestations, as clear vision and divine spheres of influence are unveiled at this time! There is nothing that has been previously out of order where complete alignment shall not take precedence, declares God. Magnanimous shifts and purging transpires to clear out every stagnant thing.

Be of a courageous heart, sound mind, and peaceful spirit, for I have gone before you to straighten everything out and the darkness shall not prevail, declares the Lord of Hosts. Be not double-minded, for a double-minded person is unstable in all of his / her ways. So, at all times, my people are to allow their no to stand as a definite no while their yes shall suffice as an emphatic yes. Choose wisely, choose the high road of what is right and just in your own life, while allowing each person to work out his / her journey in spirit and truth.

What do light and darkness have in common? Absolutely nothing, declares God. Whenever light enters the room or any place, then the darkness must flee because everything that is done in and out of darkness shall be brought to the light and exposed for the wickedness, contention, and vileness thereof.

Be of steadfast faith while knowing that the promises of the Lord your God unto you shall not return void. Now is the time to prioritize all matters by way truth and honesty. Let the redeemed of God Almighty stand up and say so because I am forever faithful to my word. I am Jehovah God – Faithful and True until the end of ages, sending forth provision to establish the visions that I have imparted into my people. Rejoice, for harvest seasons have arrived.
Amen

Saturday Morning {*dark hours*}
08 November 2003 @ 0355 Hours

All praises, glory, and honor unto the Lord thy God, for great is the faithfulness and grace. On this day and in this very hour- while most of humanity sleeps, God is alert and alive- not just now, but all the time! Faithfulness is the account for this day, declares God. The people that I have called according to my Holy Name are required to make decisions that shall shape and mold the rest of their lives, says God. Behold! This is the critical moment of choice as my people have come to these pivotal forks in the road, says God. Although both ways look equally safe, the wrong choice and path shall surely lead to chaos, death, and destruction. Therefore, the people are encouraged to seek wise counsel through me- Jehovah God, so that they will be led into the right direction and plans that are best for their lives, says God. A fool in his/ her folly self-destructs. Therefore, be not in close proximity of those who shall get swallowed up through waywardness, confusion, and strife, and discord, for those who have no regard for their own lives have not concern for the well-being of others.

Today is a day of miracles, breakthroughs, and Divine Interventions. So, be on point for amazing setups, and on guard to protect the visions that have predestined for your lives, says God. After today, nothing shall be the same again and those who are broken shall not leave the same way they entered into My Presence. Divine Timing and Supernatural Manifestations are bearing much fruit. Expect the delightfully unexpected, while preparing for awesome encounters through spiritual awakening and rebirth.

I -Lord of Hosts hereby declare that every assignment of darkness and curse of the enemy has been broken. Take no consideration for the battles that have already been won, for surely, I have gone out before you to set the houses in order and caused all things to be favorably positioned, proclaims God Almighty. The people of truth and wisdom are to prepare for miraculous waves of refreshment, as their dwelling places being overtaken by grace untold within next 72 hours. Therefore, my people are to examine and release their words carefully because whatever they produce-- that shall become the harvests they will feast upon.

There is a divine shifting in the spirit realms, becoming tangible and evident in the natural, soon to be revealed. Furthermore, those things that my people have wept over, prayed for, and fasted over are being hand delivered in freedom and abundance, says God. The enemy is dead on arrival, so rejoice, as I have covered you from every possible angle.

The ways have been made for new homes, yet only unto those that have proven as faithful stewards where they currently abide. The processes shall be painless, as the Holy Spirit has gone out before you and secured the best properties available for my people at discounted prices! Provision has been made for all needs through me, for I alone am Jehovah God and great is my faithfulness indeed!

Amen

Sunday Afternoon
09 November 2003 @ 1630 Hours

Shout Grace, Grace! For the mercy and ever-abounding grace of the Lord floods light into all the dark places and set the captives free. Many are bound and stranded out in the wilderness because they have not seen true light in so long until they have acclimated to the darkness, says God. Therefore, they have learned how to maneuver in the darkness and their means of survival have been adopted as normalcy. Make no mistake; the Holy Spirit comes to illuminate the darkness and creating space for the Light of Almighty.

On this day, proclaims God- I am preparing my people to take dominion and authority over their spaces of influence. Yet, they must first become accountable for serving as faithful stewards over the primary things that they have been blessed and empowered to be caretakers of. If the people's housing and dwelling places are continually in disarray and clutter, they cannot expect to receive greater things from the Lord of Hosts. In order for the people to inherit new territory, they must be dutiful caretakers of the territories that they already possess. Moreover, whatever a person thinks, so does he / she become! Proactive changes come by way of mindset renewal, and a wiliness to examine all things, then the purging out of that which is antiquated and not conducive to the expansion of their borders and broadening of their horizons. They are to uproot negative thought patterns, while laying aside all hindrances, blocks, and every limitation that they have ever placed upon themselves. Transformation and growth are continual works in process.

God's amazing grace has kept us thus far and grace will lead us on. The abiding presence and spiritual truth come to wipe the slates clean, while setting the captives free. *Amen*

Monday Afternoon
10 November 2003 @ 1330 Hours

The unmerited, abounding Grace of God covers, restores, and brings about healing unto the soul. Nothing shall separate us from the love of God, for divine love is unconditional and without limit. Perfected Love casts out fear, whereas fear brings about torment and anguish.

At this very hour, the chains of bondage are being broken through the renewing of the mind. Therefore, who shall take a stand up for what is right when they witness injustices being poured out upon others? What do light and darkness have in common? Absolutely nothing! Therefore, darkness and light cannot cohabitate, for one can overpower and overshadow the other. The overpowering force is contingent upon which is stronger. The light shall only stay lit for as long as there is a fuel source to sustain it, declares God. Henceforth, the parable of the wise and foolish maidens: The foolish maidens did not bring enough oil for their lamps so that they could stand watch through the night for the bridegrooms to arrive. They grew tired of waiting, their lamps began to flicker out, then attempted to borrow some oil from those wise maidens who had prepared in advance by bringing extra oil, for they knew not the hour of the night the groom would arrive.

The wise maidens made a steadfast commitment to stay their posts of duty, being steadfast watchkeepers on the wall throughout the night, while refusing to give their fuel / oil to the foolish maidens, for they knew they must keep their own lamps burning through the night as to not miss the arrival of Greatness. The wise maidens advised the foolish maidens that had they not been lazy, and having brought barely enough to get by, they would have had enough to sustain them throughout the long hours of the night watch. Therefore, the wise maidens were awake, alert, and illuminated the darkness to light the way for the groom. The foolish maidens forfeited their opportunities and were bypassed, as they rejected sound instruction, wise counsel, and failed to prepare. They desired only a quick return on their stakes. *(Moment of Meditation)* ... Therefore, at all times, let your light shine among humanity, while keeping your hope fueled and spirits fed through the guidance of Spirit Divine, so that your lights will not dissipate in the darkest hours, says God.

Dare not conform to the ways of global collective for the sake of acceptance nor approval, yet become transformed through the renewing of your minds, declares the Lord of Hosts. In this day, prepare for the unexpected, as breakouts and overflow seek you out like mighty floods sweeping away everything in the paths, says God. Remain steadfast and diligent, as to not grow weary in doing what is right and necessary, for your changes and harvests are about to arrive suddenly, says God. Let the redeemed of the Lord God Almighty stand up and say so. Those who were blind shall now see the light, repent for all transgressions, and step into the positions of valor and honor for their lives, says God. Remain faithful and trusting in the Lord of all Creation, for nothing shall separate you from the Love of God. Restoration, renewal, reformation, and repair takes place from the inside out, says God.

Amen

Wednesday Morning
12 November 2003 @ 0615 Hours

All praises be unto God Most High! Today is a day of
supernatural interventions, miraculous setups, divine
visitations, and unprecedented appointments, says God. On
this day, no stone shall be left unturned. I am the Lord thy
God that sustains and heals you, abiding within the well
springs of your being. Regardless of what was said and done
yesterday to wear you down and discourage you, I shall do a
complete turnaround, making all things work together for
your good. Therefore, expect nothing but the highest favor,
rectifying those things that seem to have gone awry. *(Moment
of Meditation)* ...

Tell the truth and shame the enemy, says God. Divine Truth
ushes in significant changes to those who have an ear to hear
what the Spirit of Wisdom utters. The words of their lips
from My Spirit have been cultivated through humility and
fortitude—inalienable grace that has been bestowed upon
their lives to set the captives free.

Go ye' to the places that you are led and prompted, bolding
doing the impossible by way of Holy Spirit Presence, for lack
of the improbable, as Grace permeates the atmosphere upon
arrival. Always uphold the truth, for my righteousness is with
you. Righteousness is not a right, but a privilege, says God.
Those who reject my people based on unfamiliarity, have
scoffed at me, declares the Lord God Almighty. They whom
sow seeds of love and faithfulness are justly rewarded.
Nothing is impossible for Jehovah God. Primary fruits of the
Holy Spirit are patience, loving-kindness, temperance,
tolerance for others while giving to those in need, and caring
for those who are unable to care for themselves. In these
things, declares God, I delight. Be not deceived by those
who possess only forms of piety through religion, for they
seek to fool humankind. I am the Lord Almighty, and I am

not mocked or ridiculed, neither am I impressed with arrogance, haughtiness, or self-indulgence. Stand before me in truth, dear people, regardless of whether the truth is good, bad, ugly, or indifferent. I am the Lord Jehovah and I take those whom the world deems foolish to confound they that consider themselves as wise in their own eyes, as well as the eyes of their peers. Standfast, for the conviction of the Lord thy God has come forth to set the records straight and the houses in order!

Amen

Thursday Morning
13 November 2003 @ 0640 Hours

Hallelujah! On this day, says God, the people that I have called by my name have been clothed in grace and the highest favor. Therefore, be of good courage, sound mind, and a pure, happy heart, for the way has been made to straighten all things out. Those that abide in the spirit of grace and gratitude, while worshiping the Lord Almighty in Spirit and in Truth shall prosper, even as their soul prospers, says God. Peace be unto thee, declares the Lord God Almighty.

My people, says God, are required to lay aside all that troubles and burden them, while praising me anyhow. I inhabit the praises from the soul, as amazing grace clothes them to weather any storm. Let they that are the redeemed of God stand up and boldly say so. It is not by might, nor by power, but by and through the Divine Spirit Consciousness that the captives are set free that the people may abide in liberty and truth.

It is moving time, harvest time, and breakout season, as mighty moves of the Holy Spirit shall shift everything and everyone out of order into Divine Position, proclaims Jehovah God. I am Almighty God- Creator over all Creation. I am not as interested in the peoples' comforts, yet more so with the condition of their hearts and spirits. If they truly abide in me through an awareness as I abide within them from the beginning to end, they are to do right unto others- for generosity and benevolence are extensions of grace unto humanity.

Be of sound mind, good courage, strong faith, and a pure heart. Then, the Lord of Hosts rewards in all efforts prompted by way of spirit and truth. Remain steadfast in prayer and devotion, says God, while standing up for what is right and just at all times. Anticipate the arrival of extreme financial blessings, according to the seeds of faithfulness that have been sown with a spirit of love. The rapid return of those exiles and runaways shall yield remarkable harvests of souls into the Kingdom of God, for they have come to the end of themselves and now reached the beginning of unconditional love, goodness, mercy, and grace. Mine grace and mercy are more than sufficient in every circumstance and situation, declares the Lord Jehovah God.

Amen

Saturday Morning
15 November 2003 @ 0745 Hours

Hallelujah! As I am sanctioned to shout Grace, Grace! into every circumstance and situation today, the Spirit of the Lord is turning everything around that was formulated for my demise, says God. Be not of weakening minds, battered hearts, or broken spirits, says God. The victory has already been won and I am God Almighty over the great and the small. I decree that you were born to triumph! It is not by might, nor by power, but by the Holy Spirit, that the fruits of abundance shall be seen record time by they that have operated according to the precepts set forth through their intimate relationship with me- the Lord God Almighty. Faithfulness and diligence are rare commodities in that few remain steadfast in yet are greatly rewarded as these foundation elements are firmly rooted, working continuously from the inside out says God.

The Sons and Daughters of the God are required to extend their steps and broaden their scopes. They who desire to excel in the purposes and precepts of God are hereby instructed to shake off all dead things that attempt to bind them and prevent them from those greater purposes and assignments for their lives. Conformity brings stagnation, yet renewal of the mind brings forth transformation and liberation- giving birth to new attitudes, new ideas, new behavior, and new partnerships / relationships.
(Moment of Meditation) ...

Rid yourselves and purge your spirits of all unfruitful things and attachments, says God. Surely, if my people are unwilling to shed that which is dead, then they cannot receive new life and livelihoods. Dearly beloved, in all things, I desire for my people to prosper and be in good health and soundness of mind, especially as their soul prospers, proclaims God.

136

Those who stand up as the righteousness of God and operate in my ways shall no longer settle for mediocrity and complacency. When there is a desire to achieve and receive what they have never had, the people must be willing to do what they have never done before! How can they expect to achieve different results if they continue to utilize the same tactics and measures that have proven unfruitful before? In me, says God, there is newness and renewal every day.

Foremost, there must be a thorough assessment and analysis conducted to facilitate maximum effectiveness. After a particular goal is assessed, then a sound business plan must be established, and later implemented. However, before the plan is implemented, it must be reassessed for holes and wise counsel should be sought and consulted, so the particular things that have escaped my peoples' eyes will be brought to light by the wise counsel. Write the vision and make it plain, believe God for provision, execute the instructions of the Holy Spirit from within, facilitate the vision by way of Divine Direction, fertilize the works by speaking positive affirmations of Life, while trusting God for the increase and planting seeds of faith for the vision. Last, but not least, praise God in the times of planting, trusting that faith and diligence shall water that which has been planted to bring forth harvests. When the harvests seasons come to fruition, devote the first and best part unto God, sowing, investing, and giving to worthy causes and individuals led, while sharing testaments of faith with others, says God. Allow the words of the mouth and meditation of the heart to prove pleasing and acceptable at all times, declares the Lord of Hosts. Pray without ceasing and forget not that the Lord your God blessed and empowered you every step of the way all, from the initial vision unto the fullness of manifestation with excellence!

Tell the truth and shame the enemy. At all times, dear people, keep your ways upright before God and humanity. A person cannot live by bread alone, but through every word that proceeds from the spirit of God. Physical bread feeds a person's body, but spiritual food-, which is the awesome counsel of God from within, allows a person's soul to flourish. In all getting, says God, seek to gain understanding so that none will be left ignorant or in the dark. As my people continue in my ways and serving as mine hands extended, they are reward graciously, says God. May the joy of the Lord your God serve as your strength and portion overflowing! *Amen*

Sunday Morning
16 November 2003 @ 0705 Hours

Hallelujah! Hallelujah! Hallelujah! All reverence, honor, and praise unto the Lord God Almighty each day, for divine grace surpasses all circumstances and situations. Jehovah God: the hope of our creation, salvation, and shelter. There is no greater life source than the breath of Creation-- calling all into existence by simply speaking Light and Truth into that which was once void and dark. God said, "Let there be light", and light shone forth. Since the beginning when Almighty God called forth Pure Light into existence, separating the day from the night, light has not ceased to illuminate the Universe. Had God not created the sun to light and heat the earth, then earth would freeze over causing every living thing to perish, never to flourish or be fruitful again. How magnificent is the God of Wonders!

On this day, declares God, I am pouring out my spirit upon all they who desire to become partakers of the fullness of grace and benefactors of the spiritual utterance. Therefore, every dead, stagnant thing may be purged from the lives of my precious people who are called to Arise- coming up higher in who they were created to be! However, they must not be hasty in pointing the finger at others, for each person is to work out his / her own salvation and soul's journey and to not become ensnared by the hidden things lurking in their blind spots. Yet, my grace and mercy are more than sufficient unto those who have a heart to do what is right. Whosoever is of stable mind, there is no wisdom in straddling the fences of indecisiveness and uncertainty. When the Spirit of the Lord has spoken to them in an audible voice and languages that they understand, they shall no longer be able to feign ignorance! No decree that I have spoken unto my scribes and prophets shall go unfulfilled, proclaims the Lord of Hosts. It grieves me when the people have chosen to remain in bondage, specifically when they have deemed it easier to dwell in darkness rather than abiding in freedom, deliverance, and peace, says God. Each person shall walk in the light as they become aware of the Light within them!

Truly, I say unto thee, never shall I leave or forsake thee. My precious people are required to leave behind everything that is not for their own well-being. When I- the Lord God Almighty require my people to pick up and move immediately, vacate a premises, leave behind hindering spirits and the contention of familiarity, and they choose to continue dwelling in mediocrity and ignorance. Foolishness breeds bitterness and contention. Therefore, they need not scoff at the messengers for delivering my messages, when they have heard the truth, yet choose to reject it. I love humanity enough to have my word spoken directly into their lives by the faithful, obedient, diligent, available scribes and prophets who seek only to abide in divine will without regard to how they are received-- caring and concerned only that God is pleased with them. *(Moment of Meditation)*

Look not to the left or to the right, but to me- God Almighty, who is your help, health, strength, and redeemer, says God. Those whom I set on the path of righteousness and worship me in spirit and truth- I always protect and defend, declares God. Although many are the afflictions of the righteous, I- the Lord Jehovah God delivers my people from them all. Be not weary in well doing, for surely you shall reap harvests if you do not faint or give up. Everything is of my appointed time, says God, so allow the Holy Spirit to be the crown on your head and the lamp underneath your feet.

The Love of God is the Truth of your Calling and substance of your Faith. Those who surround you with professions of love, yet have no actions to fortify the words, then consider the words empty and allow them to fall upon deaf ears, says God. Therefore, be not moved by flattering words, yet require that their speech and actions come into conjunctive alignment on every accord. Those who love with the true heart of God-- shall treat others accordingly, not forsaking the truth by way of mistreating and abusing people. The words of their lips shall produce fruitfulness in spirit and in truth. When ones' actions are not in alignment with their words, then weigh the cost to determine whether the relationship serves as an asset or liability, declares the Lord of Hosts. Peace and Grace overflowing be unto you always, and moreover in this very moment!

Amen

Monday Morning
17 November 2003 @ 0605 Hours

The abounding grace of God is the sustenance that balances us, while making provision in times of weakness and distress. Grace and mercy carry us, as faith inspires us to strive onward even when everything seems to be coming apart at the seams and unraveling from the corners. The corners are where two points or even four points meet. When one is in a corner, says God, either their face is to the wall, or their backs are against a wall. As my people are facing the walls, they have turned their back to the enemy while seeking the face of God Almighty to deliver and empower them, gracing them with courage to turn around and face their enemy head on, declares God. When my people have their backs against the wall, says God, they have usually been pushed or backed into a corner by opposing forces. Therefore, the only way to escape the snarls, threats, and intimidation of the adversary, is to push forward without fear, while coming out swinging in full attack mode, thus turning the tables, and trapping that which has tormented them into the corner.
(Moment of Meditation) ...

As the people of God now have the upper hand, they are now positioned to become the intimidator, making advances to become triumphant in the fight. While being clothed in truth and refusing to give up, the vigilant Sons and Daughters of God are protected from the hidden weapons of darkness that would have otherwise been used to behead them. Spiritual warfare tactics, military strategy, and guidance of the Holy Spirit is what sets the warriors of God in covered places so that they shall continue to live another day, while not being slain by their own swords. Furthermore, says God, unto they who placed their faith, hope, and trust in God, the victory was secured even before the battles ever begun, whereas the fights were fixed, they simply needed to show up without fear. I am the Lord of Hosts and never do I leave my people ignorant or in the dark- especially in times of trouble yet equipping them to overtake the adversary through prayer and practicality.

On this day, says God, I am pardoning my people to grasp hold of a greater faith, also to trust in me more than they do their circumstances and situations. I AM God-- your rock in weary lands and shelter in times of storm. Now faith is the substance of things hoped for and the evidence of things not seen. Faith comes by hearing and hearing by the presence of fellowship in God, declares the Lord of Hosts.

Be not weary in well doing, for surely you are due to reap your greatest harvests yet! Regardless of how the dilemmas appear or what they may feel like, I- the Lord your God shall do new and quick works to turn everything around in your favor that has come against you. Boldly proclaim those things that I have said and surely, you shall see the goodness and grace of the Lord thy God in the land of the living without fail.

Although you have exhausted your mind trying to figure out this quagmire and foolish situation, says God- I have already set an expiration date on the madness and mayhem. Just rest and abide in me, knowing that I am Lord over all or master over none. Choose ye' this day whose report you shall believe and what master you shall serve. The provision has already come forth through my grace! Rejoice! Rejoice! Shout unto the Lord thy God, as mercy, love, grace, and power covers and supplies from head to toe.

Amen

Tuesday Morning
18 November 2003 @ 0550 Hours

Glory Hallelujah! All thanksgiving and praise unto the awesome Jehovah God, for He is the "Great I Am"! God is up to something phenomenal in this present season. This is a day of prime positioning, says God. Therefore, suit up in my entire armor so that mind, heart, body, and spirit are on one accord-- girded in truth and clarity by way of Spirit, whereas you are being released from worry, anxiety, and stress. In all things, be anxious for nothing, for each day has enough troubles of its own. As my precious people stand in faith, they are to be of stable mind, eternal praise, and emphatic thanksgiving, regardless of whether they are abasing or abounding. After having stood boldly and confidently on the words that I shall speak unto them, says God, surely, they are being clothed in perfect peace, as they keep their hearts and minds focused on the faith of their calling. So, be steadfast in prayers and intentions, while focusing only on those things that are pure, righteous, true, and edifying and of a good report.

Now is moving time, declares God, and everyone and everything that stagnates when I have required them to move is being leveled. Make all requests known unto me through prayer and supplication, foremost honoring the God of Creation, and worshiping the divinity of spirit and in truth. Those who are wise stewards over all that has been placed into their hands, nothing essential is withheld from them. My people are to guard their hearts and do not become enablers of those who continue seeking the easy way out. Enablers will be held accountable for providing quick fix solutions to ongoing problems of the foolish. Not everything that I place into my peoples' hands is meant to be released to every by-passer who desires the blessing- while refusing to exercise their faith and working towards establishing an intimate relationship with God by way of spirit consciousness, that causes them to become enlightened and empowered. Advise them that because I am your source, you are not their source. They too must come to learn my ways and precepts through communing and fellowship, by going deep to become filled with wisdom and revelation knowledge.

They who rebuke and scoff at the truth abide in rebellion. Therefore, my people are not to become offended when others grow angry with them. Those who dwell in anger-- they lack both discipline and self-control, says God. I have imparted into you the spirit of truth. Those who worship me in spirit and in truth are required to tell the truth, the entire truth, the unadulterated, unpopular truth, which brings many to a place of unrest. They who are uncomfortable with Divine Truth may easily show themselves as an enemy rather than a friend. I am the Lord of Hosts, and have no interest of nursing their hurt feelings, yet more concerned with the condition of their souls, mind, heart, and spirit. Those who reject the truth by way of Spirit, push away and forfeit magnanimous blessings for their lives.

Shout hallelujah and grace into every situation and circumstance. This is a day for receipt of Divine Impartations, says God. Grace, honor, and praise unto the Lord Jehovah—for I AM Almighty God boldly declaring the beginning from the end and the end from the beginning! Praise the Lord for a peace that surpasses all understanding. On this day, all provisions have already been made and there shall be no stone left unturned!

Amen

Wednesday Morning
19 November 2003 @ 0935 Hours

Hallelujah! The spirit of the Lord God Almighty abides
heavily upon the place where I dwell--paving the way for all
things out of order to become rightly aligned by way Spirit.
There is nothing impossible for me, says God. At this very
hour, I have impressed upon the hearts and spirits of many to
pray and intercede for you and my vision for your life. Not a
single drop of grace shall be withheld because as you have
been shown the Greatness of Vision with spiritual eyes, you
have arrived at crossover point where the awesome wonders
in full bloom are being manifested. Therefore, prepare to suit
up in the fineries that are to be provide, for this is a season of
Divine Visitations and Supernatural Impartations, declares
God.

Tell the truth and shame the enemy, for even the enemy
knows when my truth is spoken, says God. No matter what
the cost, it has been paid in full. The exiles, runaways, and
outcasts are being led out from the yokes of captivity and
slave mentality- beginning NOW! No stone shall be left
unturned. How can one enter the strong man's house and
plunder all his possessions unless they first bind up the strong
man? If the strong man is not first bound, then he/ she will
stand in dominion and exercise authority to protect his / her
household when imminent dangers to their loved ones and
home is under threat!
(Moment of Meditation)

Write the vision and make it plain, says God. Be still and
know that I am the Lord thy God!! This is the day for
miracles and breakthroughs, by the workings of the Spirit
Consciousness. The powers of darkness shall not prevail
over you. Rest assured that in all things, as you devote
yourself to prayer and diligent works, all things needed are

being provided for. Now, let the redeemed of the Lord God Almighty boldly stand up and say so.

Love the Lord thy God with all your heart and soul, trusting that all provision is made available without delay. Supernatural release has been decreed on this day, declares God. Rejoice, as the goodness, grace, and mercy of God endure forever.

Amen

Thursday Morning
20 November 2003 @ 0710 Hours

Hallelujah! Glory and honor unto the Lord God Almighty, for he has decreed this day and season for sudden, divine change! Though the earthly seasons change gradually, the shift in the cosmos creates supernatural immediate changes in the life seasons of people. Therefore, stand in expectancy of quick manifestations, says God. Although they may appear quickly, do not mistake these things for microwave miracles, for they have been delayed in the spirit realm for long durations. These things shall appear as sudden rain showers. Although the rain was not expected, anticipated, or even deemed likely, says God, I shall open atmospheric windows and doors, causing the clouds to burst open, yielding abundant moisture upon those who worship me in spirit and truth and have proven faithful. Now, new wine and fresh outpouring of the grace comes forth, declares the Lord of Hosts. This is the day for those dry bones that once flourished to be called back to life, becoming fruitful and multiplying. In all things, give praise and reverence unto the Lord thy God, for the giver of life has made all things new.

Take heed of they who appear to walk upright, but harbor the spirit of resentment, contention, unjust anger, sowing seeds of discord among the brethren, malice, compulsive control disorder, gossipmongers, and slothfulness in the ways of doing what is right. They look among their brothers and sisters to determine and assess what others have, while comparing their livelihoods to that of their peers. The rewards of faith and faithfulness in adhering to what is right yields fruitfulness.

Be not ruled by the flesh, says God, for the flesh is simply the packaging and selfish nature in which the soul and spirit resides. Nothing can be poured into a closed jar. If a jar is already full and not pouring out its contents into others, then surely anything additional poured into it would be a waste and go unused, declares God Almighty.

No matter what the circumstance or situation, faith and perseverance create capacity for expansion. Therefore, let not the opinions of others determine how one exercises their faith. Nothing is hopeless, providing hope and faith the Lord Jehovah God is present. Know and trust that I am the Lord your God now and forever more.

Amen

Friday Night
21 November 2003 @ 2350 Hours

On the brink of this new day, says God, I will show myself faithful on every accord and they that have spitefully abused and wronged my people will be made to come full circle and bring forth recompense. They will not be allowed to sow sparingly, however will have to empty out their pockets, purses, and wallets to assure that my peoples' needs are met whom they have wronged. Yet, this is not for the faint at heart. This is primarily applicable to those who have worshiped me in spirit and truth, while having sown in tears and blood through adversity.

This is a season of Divine Change and supernatural outpourings, says God. Prepare yourselves for the inheritance and harvests of many fields and vineyards. Let the overflow begin to pour out right now! I am God, the creator and giver of life. I am the Lord of Hosts and graciously rewards those who are diligent and available in that which they have been assigned. Everywhere the soles of your feet tread, it is being granted as new, remarkable territory, says God. Hearken my voice and heed my call. In the same measure that my people have sown with purity of heart, it shall be given back to them in overflow and abundance, declares the Lord of Hosts.

Out of the ruins, declares God-- emerges steadfast, bold waves of spirit wisdom and divine order, that shall torch false doctrines and shaky, chaotic foundations to rubble, says God. Henceforth, I- God Almighty, by way of spirit, shall appear in rare form, using mightily they that have been by-passed and stepped on to proclaim my word. Rejoice, declares God. Yet, REPENT for unfruitfulness. Seek me first in all things and I shall rain down my goodness and mercy to they that have first sought my presence and heart- not my hand! Behold, for renewal, restoration, unity, and peace is released--

setting up new world order, in the establishment of Greater Good unto all.

Amen

Saturday Morning
22 November 2003 @ 0530 Hours

Blessed is the name of the Lord thy God forever more. Hallelujah anyhow, even though it makes no sense to the natural mind. Hallelujah anyhow- regardless of how the circumstances and situations appear. Hallelujah anyhow- despite the suffering, struggles, and abasement. Hallelujah anyhow- for everything that we see now is subject to change suddenly, declares the Lord of Hosts! Hallelujah anyhow- even if you do not have a firm grasp on the next provision, next meal, next bus fare, next time you will have more than two cents in your pocket, the next monies to pay the rent or secure whatever is needed, yet not lacking in faith. Hallelujah anyhow! Hallelujah anyhow! Hallelujah! I am the Lord thy God and as surely as you have proclaimed Hallelujah Anyhow, I pour out my abounding grace and mercy without limitations, along with supernatural favor of the Spirit Divine to invade all situations! Therefore, look not to the left or to the right, but to the Lord your God- which comes your health, help, and strength. For the grace of God covers every dilemma.

No matter where you have been, says God, and how low you are, none of it shall compare to where I am taking you. You have walked when you had no other mean of transport, you have carried on when you had not strength left, you have prepared a gourmet meal when the cabinets were nearly empty, and you have abided in faith until you have been pressed to move, says God. In all of these things, grace and mercy still showed up, says God. I create ways out of dead ends. I am your rock in weary lands and shelter in the times of storm! Stand still and see the goodness and salvation of the Lord your God in the Land of the Living. Right now, you must believe and holdfast to this message by faith, for there are no other available options in sight, says God.

In all things, be anxious for nothing because I- the Lord your God am already aware of your every need and the way has been made. Rest assured that you shall see me show up right where you live suddenly and immediately, says God. My truth shall never return to you void! Allow others to have their say, yet you must hold onto your God who always has the last report. You are required to walk by faith and not by sight and lean not to your own understanding. Stand on the word of God, for my promises are yes and amen unto those who are adherent to my call.

The people that I call by my name, shall be brought forth as pure gold—through the process of being put into the fire to purge out all impurities, refined and enriched unto the highest standards and specifications, says God. I have poured my spirit into them and now shall flow rivers of living water, declares the Lord of Hosts. Prepare for the overflow right now because this has been the most barren place that you will ever see. Therefore, kiss the lack goodbye and yield yourself to the Holy Spirit so that I may bring thee to abundant fields. Expect love offerings today for on the winds come increased finances, while divine visitations are to be anticipated, says God.

Amen

Sunday Morning
23 November 2003 @ 0845 Hours

Hallelujah, hallelujah, hallelujah! All praise, glory, and honor unto the Lord Jehovah God. On this day, declares the Lord of Hosts, my grace is more than sufficient unto you. The time has come where all shall recognize exactly whom my people are that abide in spirit presence, communing at the table on a daily basis, to receive fresh impartations of wisdom and empowerment to touch the lost and confound the worldly wise. As my people who worship in spirit and in truth offer up sacrifices of praise and thanksgiving, overflowing measures of whatever is needed has been supplied. I am the Lord of abundance. Even in the midst of adversity, those who worship in spirit and truth shall shout **Hallelujah Anyhow!**

The way has already been paved for Divine Appointments, as my precious ones have proven faithful in the tasks that I have assigned to them, proclaims God. Therefore, expect supernatural impartations and grace abounding. At this very hour, believe me at my word, knowing that I speak not to the natural mind, but to the spirit of God within you. For truly I say unto you, the deep seeks out greater depths to pour into, says God. Let not your hearts be troubled because the battles have been won and the spoils are being delivered.

In all of thy getting, seek to gain understanding, and know that goodbyes are not for good, and farewells are not forgotten, says God. I shall place my people as a fresh thought on the hearts of those who desire to know me more intimately. I am the rock in weary lands and shelter in the times of storm. This is a day that I- the Lord thy God have made, and you shall rejoice and be glad in it. I shall provide everything to meet my peoples' needs now and forever more, when they seek first the wisdom and truth of my kingdom, declares the Lord of Hosts. I am the Lord that heals— sending forth spirit o minister to all hurts, pains, and woes.

154

Regardless of what anything looks like, says God, praise me anyhow and I shall show my faithfulness repeatedly as mercy and grace endures forever. Behold the salvation and glory of the Lord your God, for my grace forever abides with you. Boldly declare of goodness to those who are of downtrodden faith and vacated hope, because as the precious people allow their light to shine amongst those that are locked in darkness; they shall serve as beacons in the lighthouse to draw the lost nearer to me. My glory eternal is not only a thing for the afterlife, but shall be manifested in my chosen, dutiful Sons and Daughters in the here and now, says God. My faithfulness shall not return void. The joy of the Lord is your strength indeed, as you abide in grace of the Lord your God forever. Rejoice! It is Restoration Time! Favor, commitment to the call, and faithfulness of the heart unlocks the abundant harvests!

Be of sound courage, peaceful heart, and clear mind, while being anxious for nothing. The countdown shall not reach the last second-- for there is a sudden supernatural release for you quickly! Expect provisions to rush into your hands immediately. Shout Hallelujah and Thanksgiving unto the Lord of Hosts.

Amen

Sunday Evening
23 November 2003 @ 1630 Hours

All praise, thanksgiving, and honor unto the Lord Most High, for overflowing mercy endures forever! I shall dwell in the presence of the Lord forever and praises shall always be lifted up. There is no other God than Jehovah God, whom is creator and sustainer over the entire universe, humanity, plant life, animal kingdom, the oceans, creatures of the seas, and fowl of the air. Yahweh is the creator of all things great and small. Therefore, there are no details of magnitude or miniscule of which God is not aware. Although we-- as vessels of God Almighty may not understand the full scope of everything, God created avenues out and solutions long before we ever saw or realized the problems, dilemmas, or quagmires. When God brings us to anything, then spirit of truth carries us through all things, providing we hold onto the faith in which we profess, pressing towards the mark of the high calling, while fainting not even when we grow tired. No matter how a thing may appear, we are encouraged to praise God anyhow, for the spirit of Jehovah Divine is far greater than every circumstance and situation.

This marks the beginning of breakout season, declares the Lord of Hosts. Where there is lack of vision and revelation knowledge, the people of God shall quickly perish. A little bit of knowledge with no wisdom always proves to be a dangerous thing. Therefore, guard thy hearts and minds against those that appear to be educated through world doctrine and mechanisms, yet having not sought Spirit Divine for the wisdom to apply and utilize the knowledge properly and effectively, say God. Seek wise counsel, my dear people, that you are not led out on a limb to be tossed out of the trees into midair, and then devoured by the vipers as soon as one hits the ground, declares the Lord Jehovah God. *(Moment of Meditation)* ...

Give glory unto the Lord --and the Holy Spirit as a Comforter and friend. Stand up to be counted as the righteousness of God, and boldly proclaim that neither the gates of darkness shall never prevail. I- the Lord God Almighty am a prayer-answering, miracle working, loved one redeeming God and there is none like me.

Be not weary in well doing, for multi-dimensional, tri-fold harvests are arriving, whereas everything that was previously delayed and denied is hereby released unto you! I am the Lord God Almighty, Forever Faithful and True. I have never seen the righteous forsaken, or my faithful Sons and Daughters out begging for bread. The provision that is needed has already been taken care of and shall come effortlessly, simply because of faithfulness. The loved ones of the people of faith are being delivered out of captivity, as those households that have established covenant with Jehovah God shall experience Divine Increase, Renewal, and Supernatural Restoration, says God.

The earth is trembling under your feet as blessings, wonders, and manifestations erupt in your livelihood like volcanoes ejecting lava flowing increasingly from the bowels of the earth. Your best is yet to come, so do not give up hope. Blessings, provision, and manifestation are enroute to you and the family, so render thanks- even before the arrival, and you shall be pleasantly surprised, says God.

Amen

Monday Morning
24 November 2003 @ 0615 Hours

Thanksgiving, worship, and honor unto the Lord Almighty-
highly exalted, for marvelous are the divine works of creation
indeed! At this very hour when all seems yet still in the quiet
o the morning, I- the Lord thy God pours out shiploads of
provision to be multiplied through the works of your hands.
No matter what circumstances and situations have looked like
previously, everything is be turned around in your favor.

Blessed are they who aim to walk upright in the eyes of God
and humanity. However, first seek to do all that is right and
pure unto others as to not hinder your blessings, declares the
Lord of Hosts. Each person is a work in continual process.
Even though some may be further along in their journey and
faith walk than others, no one has arrived! When they fall,
they are encouraged and required to get back up again, not
wallowing in their shortcoming or missteps. By faith, all
things are made possible unto those who believe.

This is the day of quick works and supernatural change unto
they that have diligently pursued truth and justice. The power
of life and death are in the tongue and the people shall have
whatever they say, while receiving whatever they profess. Be
careful at all times that the words from ones' own lips are not
producing death and stagnation in the lives of themselves and
others. More often than not, declares God, the people
become ensnared by the fruit of their own lips. Therefore,
with the assistance of the Holy Spirit, they are to carefully
examine and monitor the words that they speak. Providing
their words do not sound pure when examined in the mind-
then they are not to allow those words to escape their lips,
says God. Whatever is good, holy, pure, lovely, edifying, and
honorable-- let those of wisdom concentrate on these things.
Abandon idle conversation, for it is not in the best interest,
greater good and common welfare of others or self, says
God. *(Moment of Meditation)* ...

158

Thirty days from today, mighty miracles, signs, wonders, and manifestations of the Holy Spirit shall be seen, as abundance freely flows in the lives of those who worship in spirit and truth, while first acknowledging the God of Creation in all their ways. However, all that was previously delayed is being released quickly! Supernatural release from the depths of the universe is currently enroute, and not a moment late. Every good and pure deed shall be rewarded unto those who have proven faithful and stand without guilt or shame—being of pure heart, renewed mind, and consecrated body, soul, and spirit. These elements are paramount in greater dimension works.

Clap your hands and rejoice, says God. Everything needed has already been provided in unusual ways and through unlikely visitors, says God. Check your mailbox quickly, for much needed help has arrived. Trust beyond doubt that seed is always provided to the givers of life and bread to those who feed others in need. Render thanksgiving and praise at all times, for gratitude keeps the channels of blessing opened. Those who have been held captive by fear, illness, and disillusionment are being released and set free as they dare to arise and proclaim the goodness of God in the land of the living! Rivers of grace flow throughout your livelihood today, whereas nothing shall separate you from the love of God.

Amen

Tuesday Morning
25 November 2003 @ 0720 Hours

Praise unto the Lord Jehovah God, for in all things we are to give thanks. Hallelujah!

Behold: On this day, my people are become steadfast in their faith—believing that which bears truth and resonating from the depths of their soul. I have not brought you to this place to leave you, declares God. Because I have cared for you continuously and provided for all needs thus far, it is my pleasure to do it again, for you have proven faithful, and most of all abiding in gratitude. Thanksgiving season should never cease in the hearts of the people, becoming mindful in the offering of thanks unto God and others in their lives always, proclaims the Lord of Hosts. Therefore, from this point on, Thanksgiving Day is not to simply be overserved as a holiday or season yet is to be adopted as a lifestyle! Now, let they that truly are thankful, offer up praise and reverence unto Jehovah God (Yahweh)-- the giver and sustainer of life, says God. Everyone living in this day, lives by way of mercy and grace. They are preserved in divine grace, and clothes in mercy and goodness enduring. *(Moment of Meditation)* ...

Divine impartations are to be anticipated today, says God, Be anxious for nothing, yet in all things give thanks. Thanksgiving and gratitude of the heart opens windows of provision and doors of opportunity! Have I not always come through for you, inquires God? Therefore, because I have done it before, I shall do it repeatedly in greater measures. Faithful is the God of Creation, so trust and believe as you hear spirit speak in the depths of your being.

Offer up sacrifices of praise and heartfelt thanksgiving from the spirit realm and you shall bear witness to goodness and grace abounding, breakthroughs, breakouts, and miracles unfold / unravel right before your very eyes, says God.

Whatsoever you ask of me this day, it shall not be denied. Anticipate unexpected visitors and you shall be grateful in that which is to come, declares the Lord of Hosts. Whosoever honors the prophets with purity of heart, they shall reap the prophets' reward. Those who are ungrateful create continual deficits in their lives., says God. The grace of the Lord is your strength.

This is a day of Divine Interventions and supernatural happenstance. The Spirit of God smooths out the rough places while uncorking those spaces that have been compressed and blocked, says God. Let not your heart be troubled, for the ways have been made plain and clear to you. As my people receive these declarations word within their hearts, its shall not return to them void. Rejoice for the deliverance and restoration of loved ones from the confines of illness and torment, while mending of broken hearts are made new. I am the Lord God Almighty and worthy to be praised!

Amen

Thursday Morning *{Thanksgiving Holiday}*
27 November 2003 @ 0907 Hours

Hallelujah! Glory unto the Lord Most High! I- Jehovah
(*YAHWEH)* honors those who seek my presence and heart,
not mine hand. There is great reward for those who are
available to spirit -- even in times of inconvenience or
nonconventional notions, says God. Regardless of what
happens, says God, know that I am Lord over all- both the
great and small. Some of my people may struggle in their
flesh yet are pure in heart and spirit. When they are of the
Spirit of God, they are commanded to become disciplined, so
that the fruits of the spirit to paralyze that which is not for
their well-being, proclaims God. Even though humanity was
created with flaws and imperfections, says God, and
sometimes venture off the paths, overflowing mercy and
grace endures forever. When they fall, they are required to
get back up again, without hiding out in shame, guilt, or
condemnation. I have justified the called and broken, while
redeeming them through the blood of the Lamb of God.
This is a new day in Creation, and all are to become thankful,
while rejoicing in it, says God.

I am the Lord your God, Jehovah over all heaven and earth.
The people whom I call by my name are to be thankful and
grateful at all times, no matter where they find themselves,
declares God. Whether they are abasing or abounding, their
footsteps are ordered along the path they are to walk.
Therefore, be not delusional, dearly beloved children of the
Highest God- for I foreknew the ways that you would go and
the places that you would be long before you were ever born.
At all times, present yourselves as living, holy sacrifices, that
all may go well for you. Lift up your hands continuously so
that the Holy Spirit may examine and edify you, that you may
be purified, and your hands are cleansed of bloodshed,
malice, evil, and all manner of wrongdoing, says God. The

love of God covers, nourishes, and supplies, extending Goodness, Mercy, and Grace unto whosoever will simply come, drink, receive, and be satisfied.

Nothing shall separate you from the love of God! Wherever there is lack of revelation knowledge and vision, the people perish. I implore thee, declares Yahweh, to bear in mind, that you are indeed your brothers and sisters' keeper. Should you stand by and watch him / her unknowingly walk into danger without attempting to warn and rescue them from the swords and snares of darkness, says God, I shall hold you personally accountable and responsible for turning the blind eye while another got devoured. Allow not this message to fall upon deaf ears, says God.

The glory of the Lord is your strength. I am your keeper, lover, kinsman redeemer, almighty provider, friend when you are lonely, healer when you are sick, deliverer when you have been bound, rock in weary lands, and shelter in times of storm. This is not the end of the story. Hold on and know that troubles and trials are but for a season and come to make you strong, while perfecting your character and faith in me. When a city has been fortified, says God, chaos mongers wreak destruction upon themselves in trying to tear down those that have been set apart as spiritual fortresses, declares Jehovah God.
(Moment of Meditation)

Hallelujah! The captives have been set free. The effectual, fervent prayers of the righteous avails much, proclaim God. In all of thy getting, seek to gain understanding. One cannot effectively battle what is not understood. The people perish for lack of revelation knowledge. Adhere to my plans and purposes for your life and you shall not eat the bread of shame or humiliation. Steadfast prayers and faithfulness, rendered with a heart of Divine Truth, sustains my people in increasing merit. Grace unto you in every coming and going, says God. Praise and thanksgiving have broken the back of the darkness, bringing everything meant for destruction to a screeching halt! The Lord Almighty is forever faithful indeed!

Amen

Dawning of the THIRD Day

Wandering through their journey –inside of those Lost Souls,
The search for Restoration, feverishly growing Cold,
Then, Divine mercy and salvation-
Serves as covering and Shelter to those without a home.
The quest for belonging, that almost escapes reach,
Listening to the voices as the apostles and prophets teach,
Of Goodness, Wealth, and Glory, so plentiful to all,
Through Grace redeemed a new order of the Third Day, even
after the Fall!
Come one; come all Obedient unto the Lord!
In Bonds of Unity, we stand on ONE accord.
Speak Light into the darkness, before each victory, came the
Storms,
Yet, THIS TOO SHALL PASS!

Thanksgiving and praise to exalt the God Most High,
Arise- for as children of the King,
Knowing our Identity and True Purpose that we were created
for,
Thus, we shall not lack any necessary thing.
Through **The BLOOD**- the price for Freedom was long ago
paid!
Those who are faithful in little things shall be blessed with
much,
In the sowing of plentiful seeds are the fruits of
Unconditional LOVE and TRUST,
Then reaping the Harvests of FAVOR and Undenied Justice!
SHALOM- {Peace, Wholeness, Nothing Missing or Broken}
For on this Day, the Lord Almighty has spoken-
And so shall it be done! _Amen_

By: C.K. Ford
Written: May 12, 2001

Final Notes:

Gratitude and Thanksgiving to all for partaking of my work, also for your willingness to embark upon your personal journey with Spirit through the reading of this book. As the curtain closes in the final pages of this particular work, it is my sincere hope that you will continue on your path to dig deeper, aim higher, and spread your wings in the many endeavors of your life. The God / Goddess within you is YOUR HOPE OF GLORY. Never give up or throw in the towel, for you are closer than your think, as you forge full speed ahead in the greatest adventures of life. Wherever you happen to be, remember—it is does not have to be over, for you can begin again from the exact place that you are. It is never too late!!

Peace, Love, and Blessings to All! Thanks so much for your generous support! If you had a good experience with **"MIRACLE ZONES"**, which is my third release, then please do me the honors of securing a copy my previous works, as listed below, currently available in Paperback and E-book: (Audio Books coming SOON !!)

"THIRD DAY REVELATIONS" :
Book 1 of The Waters of Life Chronicles

"SILVER SHADOWS of the MOONLIT SOUL"

Ms. C.K. FORD-

www.CKFord.Online

Stay tuned for more exciting projects to come by following my work via Author's Central Page on Amazon!

ABOUT THE AUTHOR:

Ms. C.K. Ford: Author, Speaker, Teacher, Mentor, Entrepreneur, and Spiritual Counselor is a native of Louisiana. Currently residing in Atlanta, GA, she has served as an advocate, supporter, and friend to the military veterans' community, at-risk youth, while having been a safe place, confidant, and voice to those marginalized and disenfranchised. Ms. Ford has worked at helping others to find their voice in the world in spaces of service and volunteerism, in addition to having served in various aspects of ministry, she is also an active and esteemed member of ***The Professional Writers Alliance***.

Ms. Ford—a Combat Army Veteran, believes that everyone has a purpose, journey, a path that is unique to who they a Therefore, she encourages each person she encounters to deep in their personal adventure of self-discovery to find their place in the world by allowing their light to shine in who they are as a uniquely gifted soul creation. Every person has value and through learning what you bring to the tables of life is priceless, thus shall enable and empower you to show up in the Truth, Authenticity, Creativity, and Brilliance of Ingenuity-- to become the best person that you were created to be!

Is. C.K. Ford has also had the opportunity to serve as an teemed guest speaker and interviewed on several lcasting shows including:
e Breakthrough Show Network",

ect Joy Podcast Live",

's Digital Café", and

uth Behind the Truth"— all serving broad ases, through worldwide streaming outlets, over dia platforms.

Interests include:

;, cooking, communing with nature, creating ing, and Self-Development.

nation and upcoming events, or contact booking as a Guest Speaker or Co-host, ving modes of outreach:

rd.Online

ıline

e.
lig

<u>Amazon Author Central</u>: **Ms. CK Ford**

Phone: (770) 927-7563

Mailing Address:

C.K. Ford Media
P.O. Box 44
Clarkston, GA 30021

THIRD DAY
REVELATIONS

Book 1 of The Waters of Life Chronicles

C.K. FORD

AUTHOR, SPEAKER, TEACHER AND LIFE COACH

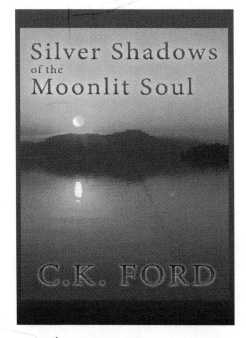

Silver Shadows
of the
Moonlit Soul

C.K. FORD